Playing for Rangers No 8

PLAYING FOR RANGERS NO 8

Edited by Ken Gallacher

Stanley Paul, London

Stanley Paul & Co Ltd
3 Fitzroy Square London W1

An imprint of the Hutchinson Publishing Group

London Melbourne Sydney Auckland
Wellington Johannesburg and agencies
throughout the world

First published 1976
© Stanley Paul & Co Ltd 1976·
Photographs © Sportapics, Syndication International

Printed in Great Britain by litho by
The Anchor Press Ltd and bound by
Wm Brendon & Son Ltd both of
Tiptree, Essex

ISBN 0 09 127480 X

CONTENTS

A NIGHT OF NOSTALGIA AND JOY AT IBROX

The players lined up to salute the newly-crowned Scottish League champions as they took the field – and forty thousand Ibrox fans roared their own salute to the 'treble' winners.

But the on-field tribute was even more moving, because the players who stood to applaud were the heroes of other generations.

Ibrox, as one writer put it the next day, had been transformed into a time machine. Incredibly Vice-chairman Willie Waddell had gathered together players from the other two treble winning seasons. From 1949 he had gathered Bobby Brown, Jock Shaw, Sammy Cox, Willie Woodburn and others . . .

From 1964 Bobby Shearer, Eric Caldow, Jim Baxter and Davy Wilson lined up with other familiar faces. There they stood, so many years apart, yet happily cheering John Greig and his team-mates onto the field for the present-day Ibrox skipper to be presented with the League Championship trophy.

It was a moment of nostalgia, one of those moments which will be remembered over and over for the contribution made by the veterans. For they didn't only stand to applaud – they played. Yes, for quarter of an hour they played a challenge game with one of the greatest Ibrox heroes of them all, George Young as the referee.

One by one they were introduced. First came the 1949 side – one which included Willie Waddell himself as well as present Ibrox assistant manager Willie Thornton. As the legendary names were read out by Waddell the crowd roared their delight.

The still golden-haired Bobby Brown was in goal, then Willie Rae and Jock Shaw as full backs; Ian McColl, Willie Woodburn and the immortal Sammy Cox, home on holiday from Canada, were the half backs. Then Waddell on the right wing, Willie Findlay, Thornton, Jimmy Duncanson and Eddie Rutherford.

Skipper John Greig, wearing the number three jersey, goes to salute the fans who massed on the Ibrox terracings for the last game gala night.

Rangers' captain John Greig is congratulated by former Scotland and Sunderland Manager Ian McColl while another Ibrox veteran from the 1949 treble team, Willie Rae, smiles in the background.

Standing by as substitutes – and they were needed!! – were Willie Paton, Adam Little, Davie Marshall and Billy Williamson.

Then came the 1964 side – Billy Ritchie in goal, still playing last season for Stranraer; Bobby Shearer and Eric Caldow; Davie Provan, Doug Baillie and Jim Baxter; Johnny Hubbard, Wilson Wood, George McLean, Ralph Brand and Davy Wilson.

It seemed the 'game' had only just started when Willie Waddell was substituted as Sandy Jardine held up the No 7 board to the laughter of the crowd. Then the 'old team' went behind when Davy Wilson made one of his famous penalty area dives and was given a penalty by George Young. Naturally, that master of penalty kicks, the little man from South Africa Johnny Hubbard scored.

Then George McLean scored another and it needed a penalty for the 1949 team to make the score more respectable. Willie Woodburn came up to score that one.

Then it was over for the fans – except for the League game with Dundee United. They stayed and they watched the two teams play out a 0–0 draw. It meant Premier League safety for United.

But for Rangers it was all a meaningless exercise. After all the championship had been won against the same opposition at Tannadice ten days earlier. The tension was gone, the hunger was off them, and the fans left still talking about the memory-stirring opener.

At the end of the game it was the same way. Upstairs, along the corridor from the Blue Room, the men who had returned from the past joined to swap tales, re-live old games, argue about almost-forgotten incidents.

George Young was happily telling the story of one of the earlier trips abroad that Rangers had made. 'We went to Minorca and that was a place no one ever went to in those days,' he recalled. 'Remember this is going back nearly thirty years. Anyway I was thinking about it because I'm going for a holiday there this year.

'It's going to be a whole lot different. Of course, we didn't fly there from the mainland of Spain, you know. We were told that we would sail across on a luxury passenger ship. You should have seen us when we arrived at the docks and found this wee boat waiting for us – it was hardly much more than a fishing boat. That was it, our transport. I'll never forget big Jimmy Smith falling asleep on the deck going across and when he wakened up there he was burned bright red on one side and white as a sheet on the other. He took some kidding about that.'

Then there was Sammy Cox, home to his native Ayrshire on holiday from Canada, and bemoaning the fact that he would still be in Scotland when Rangers played in Toronto on their close-season tour.

The last time Rangers had played in Toronto had been nearly a dozen years earlier. I'd been with them and Sammy had been with the team at the two matches, against Spurs and Fiorentina of Italy. He'd been in tears as the players left the Royal York Hotel that day . . .

Now, here he was at Ibrox, suddenly discovering that Rangers were heading for his home town. 'I won't be there,' he explained to Jock Wallace, 'I just can't get back in time.'

Skipper John Greig, holding the Championship trophy, makes a
lap of honour at Ibrox followed by his team-mates, before the
last game of the season against Dundee United.

Wallace was joking – 'We're going three thousand miles to see
you and you won't be there? How can that be?'

And Cox mournfully replied – 'If I'd only known earlier I
could have changed this holiday. How can Rangers be in Toronto
and I won't be at the game. It's not right! !'

But it was and Sammy had to settle for champagne poured
from the glittering Scottish Cup and the memory of being back
at Ibrox and back in front of the fans for one night only.

It was a room charged with emotion that night as players who
hadn't met for years took up where they had left off. The stories
grew better . . . the games were played over and over again . . .
and the celebrations rolled on until after midnight.

It was that kind of night. A night of nostalgia for so many and
a night of joy for the fans on the terracings who had seen heroes
from the past share the stage with the heroes of the moment.

It was a gala day which provided a fitting finale to the season
of success.

Rangers' vice-chairman Willie Waddell – one of the members
of the first treble team – takes over as announcer at the Ibrox
gala night.

THE WAY WE WON THE TREBLE by Jock Wallace

It was a couple of days after the gala night at Ibrox. Manager Jock Wallace was relaxing in his office, trying to wind down after the excitement of the 'treble' victory. A pile of letters and telegrams littered his desk, streams of well-wishing visitors filed in and out – some from as far off as Australia.

It had been Rangers' year and Wallace's year too and the fans were paying their homage. Somehow, though, between the visits and the constantly ringing telephone we found time to talk.

And it was in this interview that Wallace talked most freely about the hat-trick of trophy wins – the victories in the League Cup, the Scottish Cup and the Championship. He opened up, talking freely about his team and about Rangers' Football Club.

I asked the questions – then simply sat back to savour the answers. . . .

GALLACHER – When did you find yourself consciously think-. ing about winning the 'treble'?

WALLACE – I was thinking about it right from the very start of the season. I spoke to the players before the season opened and I spelled it out to them that far back. I pointed out that we had won the League Championship the year before and if we were good enough to win that then we were good enough to lift all three of the big ones at home.

What I wanted to drive home to them was that we had earned success and now we had to live with that success and grow with it.

We had to keep our feet on the ground, not get carried away with one title and so I told them I wanted more. I meant it too, by the way. I could sense that they were still improving, that

Manager Jock Wallace embraces skipper John Greig at Hampden after Rangers had clinched the hat-trick of trophies with their Scottish Cup victory over Hearts. Wallace says 'Greig is as great as any of the Rangers greats from the past.'

13

Martin Henderson, one of the players Wallace brought into the team last season, has Andy Lynch looking apprehensive in this scene from an 'Old Firm' clash. The Celtic full back looks in a bit of bother!

there were more victories in them. I had seen signs of that on the close season tour.

GALLACHER – Were you worried that the team would fail you around that time of the season when you lost to St Etienne and dropped a few League points as well?

WALLACE – We did win the League Cup then, of course. Don't forget that. But you're right, the League results worried me a little. We weren't doing as well as I had expected. We weren't doing nearly as well, either, as I thought we should be doing. We had to get ourselves back on the rails again and so a change or two had to be made in the composition and in the playing pattern of the team.

Johnny Hamilton was one of the players who came in and he stayed in and I think he has proved me right in picking him then. We hadn't been scoring goals either at the same rate we had scored them the year before. It was another problem at that time . . .

GALLACHER – Basically the three players who were brought in were Alex Miller at the back, Johnny Hamilton in the middle of the field and Martin Henderson up front – these were the major changes, weren't they?

WALLACE – Yes, they were, though there was a fair bit of shifting things around done as far as the playing pattern was concerned. We made alterations there as well, remember. It isn't always as simple as changing personnel.

GALLACHER – OK, that's accepted. Still, the changes were made and the players came in. Were you worried about bringing these lads in at all?

WALLACE – Well, Alex Miller, he'd been over the course before, so to speak. When we won the title Alex Miller had been in for about half the games. Remember Greigy was injured and missed matches and it was Alex who took over. So he had won a League medal and had proved himself as far as I was concerned.

Derek Johnstone – Wallace says he is 'the best player in Britain' – causes trouble in the Motherwell defence. Goalkeeper Stewart Rennie is looking on as Joe Wark races in to save the situation.

I'd no fears for him at all because he had shown his character the season before. He is a determined laddie and he works hard at the game. He improved a whole lot with playing in the first team and he'll improve still more. There are one or two aspects of his game that he has to work on – but he'll do that because he wants to be a better player.

GALLACHER – How about Johnny Hamilton, then? He was almost untried as far as the first team were concerned. You'd signed him on a free transfer from Hibs and he hadn't broken through. Did you think you might have made a mistake signing him?

WALLACE – No, not at all. He was doing a job for us in the reserves with the younger players. Actually he had been playing more in the back four than anywhere else for them – as a 'sweeper'. He deserved the chance, though, when it came. I wanted to use him and he lived up to my expectations. Hammy knows he has to keep it going, or he will be out. But he has done it and he has a lot of skill to offer. His passing helped settle the team a lot. That's the job he had to do and I was happy with him. Admittedly he did have to wait a long time for his chance but you have to give him credit. When the chance came he took it and he held onto it.

GALLACHER – And Martin Henderson?

WALLACE – Well, it wasn't luck that he was on the bench the day Derek Parlane broke his collar bone. We had had our eye on him for a while. There were signs there the season before and that's why he went on tour with us around the world. That helped him. He scored a few goals in these games and gained experience. Actually when Derek was injured he had dried up a bit as far as getting goals was concerned. It was funny, you know. There he was playing well week after week – but the goals just weren't going in for him. Martin came in and he did get a few goals which also helped his confidence. He was on the verge of the breakthrough before Derek was hurt. The way it is at Ibrox we try to gauge when a player might be ready to go with the first team, then when he might be ready to stay in the team. We were bang on the button with Martin. He went on tour and showed us what he was made of in Canada, New Zealand and Australia. Then at home he helps us win the treble. That can't be bad for a nineteen year old boy.

GALLACHER – That's covered the fresher faces – how about the player you praised most of all last year? How about big

16

Derek Johnstone, the player you claim is the best in Britain. What makes you think that?

WALLACE – That's easy to answer. Derek Johnstone is the one player in the whole of Britain who can do a different job for a team every week and do all of them magnificently. You play him up front – he gets you goals. You play him in the midfield – he adds power to any team there and still gets goals. You play him at centre half – and you have a world beater!

That's the way I look at the big fellow. Sure he had a wee bad spell last season at the start and I was criticized a little bit for standing by him.

Don't forget, though, at the time he was still scoring goals for us. It was simply a question of form. There was nothing wrong with his fitness or anything else. He had a form problem and I played him through it – and all the time he kept popping in goals. Probably because I believe in his ability so much I persevered a little bit longer with him than I might have done with other players.

I see him as the new John Charles, the kind of player who comes along only now and again, and who can play well literally anywhere. Charles was that way and there was the fellow with Leeds United, Paul Madeley, too. He could play in a few different roles – though he doesn't reach the high standards Derek has. The big man has class. Look at the way he kept scoring goals until he overhauled Willie Pettigrew of Motherwell to be joint top scorer in Scotland. Then remember how superbly he played at Celtic Park when he was at centre half. He strolled through that one. There is no one in Britain who can match him and there are a few people who agree with me on that!

GALLACHER – Moving away from players for the moment, just how hard was it to win the new-styled League this season? Was that the most difficult of the three trophies to win?

WALLACE – I think so. The way the Premier League is built means that it must be a very, very difficult League to win. We have only the top ten teams playing in it and we have to play each other four times – that means a whole lot of hard, hard matches to win if you are to be successful.

We went unbeaten for a long, long time before we eventually overtook Celtic at the top.

I think that we would have gone to the front in almost any other League in the world with the kind of run we put together. And we knew we just had to keep on winning because we had to wait for a Celtic slip. Back about February we were behind them by a point and on goal difference as well. OK, we knew that we had to play them still, but it was tight. The great thing for us was that we finished strongly. Most years since I came to Ibrox the team have finished the season strongly – not always successfully, mind you, but powerfully.

This year was no exception and we seemed to gain momentum as every League match slipped by.

GALLACHER – How much of a success did you find the Premier League?

WALLACE – It was a hard League to play in, there's no doubt about that, and increased competition means better games. I honestly believe that the games last season were of a higher standard and that this will continue. Look at the season just gone – nothing was decided until the last couple of weeks. Until then we knew St Johnstone were relegated – but nothing else. Then we won the League title, Hibs beat Motherwell for a place in Europe and with the very last kick of the ball Dundee United drew at Ibrox in our final game and that meant Dundee went into the First Division. It was incredible. The fans like that type of thing, they want a League to be tough. They want to see meaningful games until the end of the season and that's exactly what they got.

GALLACHER – The one disappointment you suffered in the season was losing to St Etienne. How do you feel about that now?

WALLACE – Really, I would have liked to get hold of the French team around February or March in the quarter finals when we were going a bit.

Instead we caught them when we weren't going so well. It was at the time I talked about earlier when we were losing League points. Still, they were a good team. I knew that from the moment I watched them in France – maybe even before that. After all they reached the European Cup semi-finals the year before when they lost to Bayern Munich – and they won their own title in that same season. That's good going anywhere.

They had a few good players, Piazza, Bathenay and Larque to name just three of them. I was impressed by them and it didn't surprise me when they went on to do well in the rest of the tournament. We had the chance of watching them in the Final at Hampden. That made me a wee bit sick because we might have been there ourselves if we had played against them the way we

Behind the Cup – filling up with champagne – just in case you didn't know, is Rangers' boss Jock Wallace as he toasts the Cup win over Hearts.

(a) 'I've got to make a change here somewhere . . .

(b) 'Come on, pay attention, you've got to alter things here.'

A look at Wallace in the dug-out as he watches his team in one of their games last year . . . and a guess at his thoughts.

(d) 'You beauty, it's starting to pay off just the way I wanted it to.'

(c) 'Go on over there, pick it up now!'

(e) 'We've done it! What a team this is.

were playing later in the season. Still, that's how it goes in this game.

GALLACHER – What was your own personal highlight from the season?

WALLACE – There are several – the Scottish Cup Final when we clinched the 'treble' . . . and the game at Tannadice when we won the League. That was special too in its own way because we had gone up there convinced that we would not be champions until the following Monday when we had to face Celtic at Celtic Park. We were in front at that stage but we did not expect Celtic to drop points to Ayr United at home. That's how it worked out though.

'The fans were going crazy all the time during the second half of our match at Tannadice because they were getting the scores on their radios. But I didn't believe it until Willie Waddell came downstairs after seeing the final result announced on the telly. That's when I went into the dressing room to tell the boys.

Then we went out to do a lap of honour.

GALLACHER – It happened once or twice in games, didn't it, that the news of Celtic losing swept down from the terracings onto the field. Does this help the players?

WALLACE – Of course it does. It lifts them that bit, they know whenever they start to go wild on the terracings that something is happening that is good for us.

The support we have is tremendous. They were great at Tannadice and then at the Scottish Cup Final they were even better. They took Hampden over for the day and we were delighted with them. They help the team. There is no doubt about that. It's a great feeling to be there in front of them, knowing that all of them would do anything just to help the club. And they have helped us, they make a contribution to winning trophies and we are all well aware of that at Ibrox.

GALLACHER – I suppose a lot of that stems from the club's tradition.

WALLACE – It does. I used to be on these terracings myself, most of the people at the club were the same. It's not just the players and the manager who make a team successful, nor just them and the fans. So many people were behind our success last season. You see we have a family at Ibrox and the women who make the tea and the groundsman who gets the pitch in order and the women who wash the jerseys – they are all involved. From the bottom right to director level, we on the playing side know their value. Without them we wouldn't be able to achieve success.

GALLACHER – Getting back to success, would it be fair to assume your next target is the European Cup?

WALLACE – No. I keep on telling you my next target is the next game. OK it would be nice to win the European Cup, nice to win the treble again, maybe rack up six or seven of them. But I don't want to get ahead of myself. As I'm talking to you now our next match is in Vancouver and that's the one I'm thinking about. They are all important to Rangers, you know.

GALLACHER – I find it interesting that you should be asked back to Vancouver so quickly – you were there playing just a year ago.

WALLACE – Aye, we were. And when we got off the plane there after a long, long flight our players went off the way we like to see Rangers' players go off. They went off wearing their club blazers and slacks, and collars and ties. We don't believe in slovenliness – and that impressed the people in Vancouver as much as our football did, I think. We won well there, too, remember. But, back to what I was saying, one of the British Columbia officials told me that he had never seen a better behaved, better turned out football team arriving in his city. That did me.

GALLACHER – Do you see that as part of the training, part of the old Ibrox tradition?

WALLACE – Certainly, I do. We have them like that when they are boys and it stays with them. Just think back to that gala day and the way the old players turned out that night. The players from 1949 and 1964 were all there and they were there because there is still a bit of Ibrox, a bit of Rangers living with them all. They loved being back and I loved seeing them all.

GALLACHER – It sounds as if you enjoyed the night as much as the forty thousand fans did?

WALLACE – You're right, I did – except that we didn't win the game to give the fans something to sing about. Apart from that it was a great night.

They were all there, weren't they – Willie Woodburn, George Young, Sammy Cox, Willie Paton, Bobby Brown, Jim Baxter, Bobby Shearer, Davy Wilson, Eric Caldow – some line-up. I'm up there among them, too, and there are some of them calling me Mr Wallace. Older men, I mean, men I used to watch when I

Johnny Hamilton, in the reserves for so long, finds out about life at the top. Here he is in the foreground joining goal-scorer Alex MacDonald in celebrating a Cup goal against Aberdeen.

was just a youngster and they're calling me 'Mr'. That's part of the Rangers' discipline, isn't it? The respect for the manager. It made me feel proud and a wee bit humble as well that night when that happened.

GALLACHER – Of course there was something else to celebrate that night too. That was when the Scottish Football Writers' Association named John Greig as their Player of the Year, wasn't it?

WALLACE – It was and no one deserved it more than Greigy. He had a bad season for injuries when we won the title, then we went on tour and from our opening game in Vancouver, right through to that last match against Dundee United, John Greig was playing in the first team. He didn't miss a game in all that time. Now it all added up to something between sixty and seventy matches for him because he was brought back into the Scotland team and made captain, too, against Denmark. He took it all in his stride and I was proud of him.

There isn't a player who epitomizes the character, dedication and hunger that every Rangers' player needs added to his skill to become a first team man at Ibrox, better than John Greig. He had to go through some lean years with the club but he battled on and he's still there to celebrate successes.

I watched him with all these older players at that gala night party and he was one of them. I'll tell you he walked tall with any one of them and there were a few players there that the fans look on as immortals. Well, as far as I'm concerned John Greig is as great as any of them. Down through the years there have been wonderful, wonderful captains of Rangers – none better than the one I've had battling with me for the past few years.

I know just how much work he put in by himself to make sure he would carry on. There were doubts expressed about his fitness when the season started – there were none at the end. He is an example to any young player. John Greig has looked after himself, trained on his own the way a boy starting in the game would do . . . and it was a fantastic achievement to play in every match to win us the treble.

The Wallace tribute to his captain ended the interview. The big, hard man image had faded slightly as he talked. Emotion had taken over and I remembered the comment of Hearts' veteran keeper Jim Cruickshank who had been under Wallace's management at Tynecastle. 'He gives you that tough impression,' smiled Cruickshank, 'but underneath it all he's really a big softie.'

What he meant was that Wallace had a heart, had feelings for his players, and most of the Ibrox men will agree with that.

MY LEAGUE CUP GLORY GOAL by Alex MacDonald

The newspapers called it the worst League Cup Final in the history of the tournament. The fans who watched from the stands and the towering terracings of Hampden went along with that, though our supporters had the satisfaction of a victory to celebrate.

Anyhow, it didn't matter to me what anyone said about the game. You see, I'd scored the only goal of the match in the second half and that was enough to take the League Cup to Ibrox. My goal had won the trophy and nothing else mattered. That was the most important goal I've ever scored for the club. Partly because it won the Cup, partly because it gave us a win over our greatest rivals, Celtic, and also because it wiped out the memory of a defeat in Europe which I blamed myself for at that time.

We had flown home from France and our European Cup tie against St Etienne just forty-eight hours before the lunch-time League Cup Final. It was a one o'clock kick off in a bid to prevent trouble at the game – and it worked because there were only three arrests out of a fifty-nine thousand crowd.

However, we had come home trailing 2–0 in the second round match and we were down by that margin because of a late goal scored by the Frenchmen. A goal which I was taking the blame for . . .

Now, of course, I realize that it wasn't all my fault. I've had a chance to talk it all out with Sandy Jardine who was also involved and he claims that he was to blame. When we came back to meet Celtic, though, I was determined to try to do something to repay the debt I felt I owed the rest of the lads. When I scored the goal then I felt I had done that.

In that game against the French champions I had played a

Rangers are under pressure in this shot from the League Cup Final. But centre half Colin Jackson outjumps Celtic's Icelandic star Johannes Edvaldsson in this attack. The other Ibrox men are Tom Forsyth and Derek Johnstone.

ball back to Sandy in the closing minutes of the game. At the time it seemed the right thing to do. Unfortunately one of their players raced in, dispossessed Sandy and went on to score. It was a tragedy because there is a great gulf between a single goal defeat away from home in Europe and a two-goal margin. And when the second blow arrived so late it seemed even worse than usual.

I was so miserable that when we first talked about it – Sandy and I – and he said he thought it was his fault, I honestly believed that he was just trying to help me out. I thought he was saying that to make me feel better.

That's what I thought when I went into the Hampden game looking for some kind of salvation . . .

Now, though, it's different. I have come to realize that it wasn't all my fault at all. Sandy has explained that when the ball reached him he could have done several things with it. He could have played it upfield, kicked it out of play, but he elected to take the onrushing Frenchman on and he lost the ball. It was a simple error of judgement.

I reckon, still, that I didn't play a perfect ball back to Sandy. But it was the pass which was the right one to make. I was always sure of that. Now I'm convinced in my own mind that if the same situation arose in a game some time in the future then I would make the same pass. It was the easy pass to make, the type of ball you look for when you are in a tense situation. Because it went sour once it doesn't mean to say that things will go wrong again . . .

Back to Hampden, though, and the misery and guilt which still hung about me as we prepared to face Celtic. After the game all those feelings had gone – lifted by that goal, the best goal I've ever scored.

A Cup winning sequence of three pictures shows the goal which took the League Cup to Ibrox and started Rangers on the road to the 'treble'.
(a) Goal scorer Alex MacDonald is flat on the ground trying to see if his header has reached goal. It has!
Peter Latchford has missed it and the other Celtic defenders are left to right, Danny McGrain, Roddy McDonald, Johannes Edvaldsson and Tom Callaghan. Tommy McLean is beside the grounded MacDonald.
(b) Now he knows – and MacDonald rises to his feet to salute the goal as the Celtic defenders slump in gloom. Again the other Rangers' player in view is McLean.
(c) Now it's joy, joy, joy! MacDonald on his knees clutches his head while Cutty Young and Derek Parlane, the two goal makers, are beside him, Parlane raising his arms to the crowd while Young is on the ground. Colin Stein races in to join the celebrations.

I've been told since that the goal looked very spectacular and I must admit that when I've seen it on the telly it has looked a bit special. At the time, though, it wasn't all that difficult. It all seemed to happen right for me. Derek Parlane carried the ball into their box and then chipped it over from the bye line. At first I thought the ball came straight over but Cutty Young actually helped it across. When I saw it I knew this was the one for me. You see I like balls coming from the right when I'm trying a header. It's one of those preferences that players have. When I launched myself into the air I knew that I was going to make contact OK and when I headed the ball I knew I had caught it just right. But, as I went down on the Hampden turf, I began to have doubts. All I saw were bodies between me and the goal and for a terrible moment I thought the ball would be blocked or deflected – then I heard the roar go up and I knew it was in the net.

It was a great, great feeling – something that's impossible to describe. I was so happy, the happiest I've been in my whole career, probably, and a load of good things have happened to me with Rangers.

Of course, it meant a lot to me, too, to beat the Celtic. I've had my bad moments against them – including being ordered off twice. Now I try not to get so involved in the game and the role I have been given lately helps me stay comparatively clear of trouble.

It used to be that I was asked to do a specific marking job in these games. I've had to go everywhere with Jimmy Johnstone, for example. Now there is nothing angers players more than suddenly sprouting an extra shadow. It becomes very frustrating and clashes are difficult to avoid. Unhappily I couldn't always avoid them and so I was in trouble. It isn't something I'm proud of but these Old Firm clashes are very difficult games to play in. I know I feel that way and most players are the same. A game against Celtic is the one where you don't want to make a single mistake . . . one where you try to give 110 minutes' effort inside the ninety minutes that you play . . . one where the fans want a victory more than at any other time during the season. The tension builds on the terracings and sweeps down onto the field. It's impossible not to feel tense.

According to all the reports that type of tension spoiled the League Cup as a spectacle. But we weren't conscious of that on the field.

You see, it all depends on the viewpoint of the people concerned. No one ever sees a game the same way as his pal . . .

And players rarely see it the same way as sports writers or fans.

I accept that the spectators at Hampden that day didn't enjoy the football which was played – but players see things differently. I have come off the field thinking a game has been poor and then found that the fans have been raving about it. In that Hampden final I remember the job I was asked to do, I remember that we deserved to win the Final and I remember, above all else, scoring the goal. Anything else just didn't sink in with me . . .

Afterwards I realized that very few people were happy with the game just as I realized that big Tom Forsyth was being heavily criticized. That criticism of the big man was out of order. Big Tom is not a dirty player. He is quite simply a very, very hard tackler. But he is a fair tackler. For me he is one of the masters of the almost lost art of tackling. Sometimes, though, because he can look clumsy he has been tagged a 'dirty player'. It's nonsense. He is a tremendous player to have in your team and it was a shame that he should be criticized the way he was after that match.

I suppose that's best forgotten. Like I say it's the goal I want to remember most from the game. It had to be a bit special to become so memorable in a season which was the best I had had since joining Rangers from St Johnstone eight years earlier.

I'm saying that, incidentally, because everyone kept telling me so and who am I to argue? I know I felt a lot more confident than ever before and so I was willing to try things that I'd been frightened to try in other seasons. Some of the reason for that was a switch which brought wee Tommy McLean over to the left side of the field to team up with me. Incidentally I like saying 'wee Tommy' because he's the one player at Ibrox I can look down on!

The Boss (Manager Jock Wallace) made the move and we settled down to playing together. I loved it. Playing alongside him is a dream and it suited me perfectly. Before linking up with Tommy my job was often enough just to win the ball and send it out to the wings. Then I had to try to get upfield and hope the ball came across to me. Sometimes it did – sometimes I made the runs and found nothing at the end of them. Now, though, Tommy and I can set up passing movements between us. We like to play one-twos and take the ball upfield that way. Honestly, you can work that kind of passing movement from one end of the field to the other with Tommy. He has a special touch and he makes it all seem so simple.

Basically I suppose it is. If you take up a good position, un-marked, then you will get the ball from him. And, of course, when you are in possession it's odds-on that he has made space for himself. He has this knack of drifting clear of opposing defenders. If he doesn't give you the ball then it will be because he has spotted someone else who is better placed than you are. He has tremendous vision and he passes the ball more accurately than anyone else at Ibrox. It's tremendous to play with him and my game improved thanks to him.

The boss helped me too, of course. He sensed that I was trying to play every minute of the game at top speed and he asked me to slow things down. He wasn't looking for hurried moves from me all the time. He told me that he wanted me to relax a little bit, to calm my game. Mind you. my problem is that I look a hurried player all the time. It's my style, I guess. Even when I think that I'm taking things easy and listening to the advice I've been given I look as if I'm rushing things. Still, I did act on his advice and I slowed things down, became a little more deliberate and there is only the odd occasion he has to pick me up on that aspect of my game now. I've known him to come into the dressing room at half time during a game and tell me – 'You're away again. You're playing the game at a hundred miles an hour . . . get it down to eighty!'

That little warning is enough to make me conscious of playing the ball too fast again. So I listen to him, do what he advises and it works!

Really, Jock Wallace has been a tremendous influence on my career at Ibrox. But, besides the Boss, I owe a special thanks to Sandy Jardine who has helped me so much. I said earlier how he talked me out of blaming myself for the St Etienne goal in France – well, that's just one of the many things he has done for me. Sandy has been around the international scene, was a member of the Scotland team in the 1974 World Cup Finals in West Germany, and with all his experience he has picked up a special knowledge of the game.

He has played with the best players Scotland has produced and played against most of the top names in world football. He has learned something from all of them, I think – or seems to have done. Believe me. when Sandy talks about the game I listen, and again he is a man whose advice is good. Sometimes we talk generally – about players, about tactics, about situations which may arise during a game. Other times, though, we talk about teams we are going to play against, about individual players we will be facing and about their approach to the game. These talks have helped improve my approach to the game. It's often the little things you pick up in these kinds of conversations that become terribly important in a match. Little things add to your knowledge and make you more of a complete professional . . .

The tremendous thing about my time with Rangers, of course,

They're on the road to the 'treble' — chairman Rae Simpson holds
the League Cup in the Hampden dressing room along with John
Greig, Manager Jock Wallace and the other players. Goal hero
Alex MacDonald is blotted out by Cutty Young's empty champagne
bottle.

is that all my ambitions with the club have been realized. I won a European medal when we beat Dynamo Moscow in the European Cup Winners Cup Final in Barcelona. And, naturally, I have every honour I could have won at home because I've helped the team win the Scottish Cup, the League Cup and the Scottish League Championship. Then towards the end of last season I was picked twice for Scotland teams. That helped me achieve a long-standing ambition – to wear the dark blue jersey of my country. OK, they weren't the biggest games, one a League international and the other a game against Switzerland. The League international meant a great deal to me though. It was a chance to pit myself against so many of the top names in the English game.

Unfortunately the game itself was plagued by call-offs and these hit our team more than they did Don Revie's side. For instance, my two Ibrox mates, Tommy McLean and Derek Johnstone were out, and Motherwell's goal ace Willie Pettigrew was also missing among others. England did without some top players too but they still had Roy McFarland, Peter Shilton, Tony Currie, Mike Channon, Dennis Tueart and Jimmy Greenhoff in the strong team they fielded.

The start of Alex MacDonald's best-ever season for Rangers. Colin Stein, back to the camera, comes to congratulate the little midfield man after he had scored Rangers' second goal in the pre-season challenge game against Hertha Berlin.

We lost the game 1–0 – Trevor Cherry scored for England after only three minutes had been played – but even with a kind of a scratch team we were in no way disgraced. That was important to people like myself who were playing a representative match for the first time. I enjoyed it. In my view we showed the English lads that there is no way they should look down their noses at our domestic football. The Premier League has raised standards in Scotland and despite all the withdrawals and the fact that no Celtic players were used because they were playing in Europe that day, we still held our own. The match meant a bit of a reunion for me with my old St Johnstone manager Willie Ormond who is the Scotland boss. He was the man who sold me to Rangers and started off the Ibrox career which has brought me so many good memories.

It was a pity, though, that wee Tommy McLean and I didn't get the chance to play together against the English. As I've pointed out Tommy and I were working well together with Rangers. Continuing the partnership at a higher level of the game would have been interesting to say the least.

Still, I have to hope that there will be another chance for us to do that. Mind you, getting a midfield position in the Scotland team is not easy.

The competition for that position is pretty fierce. I watch these English games on the telly every weekend and in most of the games there's a Scot right at the heart of things. At Manchester City there's Asa Hartford, at Manchester United, Lou Macari, at Derby it's Archie Gemmill, at Newcastle, Tommy Craig, with Wolves, Willie Carr – and all of them about the same size as yours truly! Among the bigger lads there are Bruce Rioch of Derby, Don Masson of Queens Park Rangers and Graeme Souness of Middlesborough. Every one of these players is influential in his team, and every one of them has been watched by Willie Ormond and most of them have been picked for one or other of his teams – either the full international side or the Under 23 squad. There isn't much room for challengers. Naturally I'd like to think I could break through but the role I've chosen for myself just happens to be the one where the international competition is at its fiercest.

Still, I was able to win two honours and playing in the full international was important. I realized the teams had been hit with call offs because so many Anglos were unavailable through club commitments – but, still, no one can take that international cap away from me. Maybe some day I'll get the chance of more. But even if I do that won't mean as much to me as the goal which won the League Cup.

That will live with me forever!

AROUND THE WORLD IN TWENTY SEVEN DAYS

Last summer saw Rangers make the most ambitious tour in the long and distinguished history of the club. It was a tour which carried them around the world . . . a tour which meant the team playing eight games in three different countries . . . a tour which brought tens of thousands of exiled fans flocking to see their heroes in action!

And, as always, with Manager Jock Wallace it was a tour with a meaning. For it was on the trek to Canada, New Zealand and Australia that striker Martin Henderson and full back Ally Dawson were discovered as first team potential.

Wallace had looked for a major overseas tour to blood some of his younger players and to build up team spirit in his squad. He had often stressed that team work was fostered best among players when they were living and working together over a long period of time.

The tour brought him twenty-seven days to work in . . . twenty-seven days which carried the team close to thirty thousand miles as they circled the globe. He broke fresh ground for Rangers, playing first on the west coast of Canada in Vancouver and then crossing the Pacific for games in New Zealand and Australia. Wallace had wanted games there because he knew from the overseas mail he received at Ibrox that the exiled Scots wanted to see Rangers playing again. To a certain extent he felt that it was the club's duty to take the players to these countries and allow the legions of still-loyal supporters to see them. Taking the team as newly-crowned League champions was a special bonus.

When the plans for the tour were first outlined the itinerary had suggested two games in Djakarta on the way to Australia.

Alex MacDonald was the first victim of the injury jinx which hit Rangers on tour. Luckily he was at peak fitness during the season at home as this picture shows. Here he jumps with Derek Johnstone to challenge Ayr United keeper Hugh Sproat. Look at the height the little man has climbed to!

Rangers, though, preferred to go to Canada for their first stop. As details of the games materialized Ibrox was deluged with cables, air mail letters, even telephone calls from all three countries as anxious fans began a hunt for match tickets. The London agent who set up the tour told me: 'We have arranged tours for almost all the top teams in Britain – but we have never known anything like the response we have had since announcing that Rangers were to visit these three countries. We have come to realize that Rangers are not simply another football club – they are an institution!'

That, of course, became even more apparent as the tour got underway. Fans travelled thousands of miles to see their team play. In Vancouver where the tour began supporters jetted in on charter planes from Toronto, that Scots-flavoured city on the other side of the Continent. It was the same in New Zealand and Australia and Wallace later admitted: 'It was tremendously emotional at times. There were people who had been away from home for years but who had stayed just as loyal as any Rangers' fans back home in Scotland. They had the scarves and the flags and the banners. They sang the songs they sing at home and we were treated like kings by them. It made all of us feel good that we were able to take them a little piece of Scotland and help them remember home.

'It was an experience that few of us will ever forget . . .'

The Scots abroad would agree with that. They saw their team again, many of them met their heroes, and warm memories of home were vividly brought to life again.

It was a tour, too, which had the fans at home avidly reading the newspapers for the results of the games. And here, in diary form, are the landmarks of that epic trip . . .

MAY 28 – Rangers fly out from Glasgow Airport on the first leg of their round-the-world trip – and they leave short of players. The reason for that is simple. Four of the Ibrox regulars, goalkeeper Stewart Kennedy, right back Sandy Jardine, centre half Colin Jackson and striker Derek Parlane are still on international duty with Scotland. The Home International Championship series is over but these four must travel to Bucharest and a European Championship game against Rumania. Consequently team manager Jock Wallace takes only thirteen players with him to Vancouver . . .

One of them is seventeen-year-old Alastair Dawson, signed two years earlier from Eastercraigs Amateurs, who has left school just in time to go on the tour. He admits at the airport: 'When I was told two weeks ago that I was making this tour I just couldn't believe it. I've been so excited that I haven't been able to think about anything else for a couple of weeks. It's a tremendous chance for me and I realize that.'

MAY 29 – The team settle into their Vancouver hotel and this so-British of Canadian cities lays out the red carpet. The fans besiege the players in the hotel with the legions from Toronto prominent among them with their distinctive Rangers' windcheaters. Other fans have come from Edmonton and Winnipeg to see Rangers play the first game of their world tour against a British Columbia Select team. As well as the fans the players meet ex-Hibs and Dundee centre half Jim Easton who is now bossing the local Vancouver professional team, the Whitecaps.

MAY 30 – There are ten thousand fans in the local stadium for the game – and most of them appear to be Scots. A sea of blue greets the Rangers' players as they line up on the new astro-turf surface.

Naturally the ground's playing surface provides a few problems for the players who are not used to the synthetic turf. Gradually, however, they adjust and at half time they lead the select side by 1–0 thanks to a goal from Graham Fyfe. After half time Rangers, now settled to the astro-turf, take command. The time change and travel doesn't affect them at all and with little Tommy McLean master-minding so many of their moves they score three more goals through Alex MacDonald, Bobby McKean and Fyfe once more. The Rangers team is: McCloy; Miller, Dawson, Greig, Johnstone, McKean; McLean, Stein, Fyfe, MacDonald and Young. The two players on the bench, Tom Forsyth and Martin Henderson get a run in the second half. Says Wallace: 'It was important to let all the lads get a feel of the ball. They needed that after the travel and the time change. The different playing surface worried us a little to start with. We had to take our time settling to that but once we did then we were able to turn it on a bit. It was good to win 4–0 and I was pleased with the way all of the lads performed . . .'

But his special pleasure comes from Ally Dawson who makes his first team debut thousands of miles from Ibrox and looks an established first team player already!

MAY 31 – The start of the long, long haul to New Zealand which will take eighteen hours. The team fly to Los Angeles where there is a stop-over, then make the journey across the Pacific to Auckland. Wallace knows that this gruelling schedule will take its toll of the players' strength but is determined to

Rangers' international right back Sandy Jardine missed the world
tour because of injury – and then, playing at home, found out
just how tough the Premier League was going to be. In this
dramatic five picture sequence you see for yourself how ruthless
defenders can be . . .
(a) The game is at Somerset Park and Jardine has played the ball
beyond Ayr defender Alex McAnespie. It's obvious this early what
McAnespie is going to do . . .

(b) McAnespie has now made contact and as the ball flies clear Jardine is heading for the ground.

(c) He's up again and obviously has something to say to the Ayr man.

(d) A flare up looks imminent between the players as Jardine complains bitterly.

(e) Now they're face to face but the battle remains one of words after a cruel tackle which was caught by the camera.

Young striker Martin Henderson grew up on the world tour –
and here he shows how he learned to handle himself as he
fights it out with Hibs' iron man Roy Barry.

start the second stage of the tour with a win over the New
Zealand Select side in the Newmarket Stadium.

JUNE 1 – There is another huge welcome for Rangers in
Auckland and they also learn that the sixteen thousand capacity
stadium has been sold out for their game. This has happened
even though the New Zealand authorities raised prices sky high
for the Rangers' visit. The price for a stand seat is more than £3
and the ground costs over £2. Fans say this is much higher than
when Middlesborough played in the city – but, such is the
magic of Rangers' name, the tickets are sold out. Among the
Scots the Rangers' party meet is Bert Ormond, a brother of the

Scotland team manager. And Willie's nephew Ian is at outside left in the select team which has been chosen to face the Scottish champions.

While the tour runs smoothly there is bad news for Jock Wallace. It comes from Rumania where Sandy Jardine has been examined by doctors with the Scotland squad and told that a groin strain will prevent him travelling to join his club. The other three Ibrox men with Scotland are fit and will travel as arranged. Meanwhile the experiments with youth continue and Wallace names Martin Henderson as striker for the New Zealand opener with Ally Dawson staying at full back.

JUNE 2 – The first game in New Zealand – and a second tour victory for Rangers! That is the story at the Newmarket Stadium where the capacity crowd see Derek Johnstone storm back to his best form and power Rangers to victory. With Tom Forsyth in defence Johnstone moves to midfield and responds by scoring two of the goals in the fine 3–1 win for Rangers.

Rangers open the scoring through Alex MacDonald, then Johnstone scores two and comes desperately close to getting a hat trick. In the game's most spectacular move he beats four men and then crashes a shot against the post.

It is a good win for Rangers and helps manager Jock Wallace mask his disappointment at the news that his international trio, Stewart Kennedy, Colin Jackson and Derek Parlane, have been delayed en route from Bucharest. They are now unable to join the Rangers' tour in New Zealand and will fly directly to Australia. That leaves Wallace with the same thirteen players for the tour's third game in Canterbury. His resources are being stretched to the limit . . .

JUNE 3 – Jock Wallace, pleased though he has been with the youngsters Martin Henderson and Ally Dawson, knows that they must be rested. He makes up his mind that he will have them on the bench for the match at Canterbury. He explains: 'Both of them have done well but we have to remember that they are still boys. The travelling is tough and they have had to combat a couple of time changes as well. These things have been as troublesome as the games so far and so the lads will get a rest. It's just unfortunate that we don't have the other players here yet. They would have helped a lot.'

JUNE 4 – For the first time on the tour so far on-field troubles hit Rangers. Seventeen thousand fans see the Scots miss chance after chance as they draw 2–2 with a tough tackling Canterbury team. The well-laid plans of manager Jock Wallace to rest Ally Dawson are destroyed eleven minutes after the game starts. Alex MacDonald is carried off with a bad ankle injury and Dawson has to go on. At this stage, too, the Ibrox men are a goal down after the New Zealanders scoring in just ten minutes. Colin Stein equalizes before half time and then John Greig scores in the second half to push Rangers into the lead. But twelve minutes from time Canterbury get their equalizer. By this time Rangers have three more injured players – Dawson, Derek Johnstone and Tom Forsyth. MacDonald, though, is worst with a suspected broken ankle.

JUNE 5 – Another country and another ecstatic welcome from exiled Scots. Hundreds of fans invade the Kingsford Smith Airport at Sydney as Rangers land in Australia. A massive banner is raised in welcome by officials òf the Sydney Supporters Club as the players leave their jet. Unfortunately some of the players and Manager Jock Wallace miss the main reception. The party has been split in Wellington because of flight problems and some of the group arrive later. The good news is that X-rays taken just before Rangers left New Zealand show that Alex MacDonald's injured ankle is not broken. A dislocation has been diagnosed. But the international three are in Sydney waiting for their team-mates and join the preparations for the first game against the Australian national team.

JUNE 6 – Jock Wallace comes right out and admits to the Australian Press that the game will be 'the most important of the tour.' He says that, knowing that injuries are still wrecking his squad. Tom Forsyth will not play, nor will goalkeeper Stewart Kennedy be available. The 'keeper has arrived with a trouble-some ankle injury. With Alex MacDonald out too Rangers are left with only thirteen fit players for the prestige clash. The Australians are set to play nine of their World Cup squad and expect around thirty thousand fans at the Cricket Ground for the game. It is one they are determined to win.

JUNE 7 – After a training session and a fruitless survey of the injuries Wallace names his team. It is a simple job in view of the injury list. Centre half Colin Jackson and striker Derek Parlane who have been shuttled across Europe from Bucharest and then out to Australia have no time to acclimatize properly. They are pitched straight into the side.

Wallace's team is: McCloy; Miller, Greig; McKean, Jackson, Johnstone; McLean, Stein, Parlane, Fyfe and Young. Once more

44

the tour babes, Dawson, who is still not 100 per cent fit, and Henderson, are the only available substitutes on the Rangers' bench. An old foe arrives to see the team, ex-Celtic striker Willie Wallace who emigrated to Australia several months ago but is not eligible to play against the Ibrox men.

Rangers are now considering the possibility of flying out another player to join the tour if the injuries do not clear.

JUNE 8 – The official expectations for the crowd are exceeded – once more the crowd pulling appeal of Rangers works. Thirty-two thousand fans crowd into the Cricket Ground for the opening game in Australia and are rewarded with a vintage Rangers' performance. They win 2–1 and both goals come from Derek Parlane. The tall striker scores one in each half and gives a memorable exhibition of striking. Australia's single goal comes from a late penalty, but they have been outclassed for almost the whole game.

Again the match seems a 'home' game for Rangers with thousands of Scots cheering them from the stands. Afterwards Wallace praises Parlane. 'His goals were magnificent,' he says. 'First he gets in a header and then in the second half he scored with a superb shot. We took time to settle again and Peter McCloy did well during our shaky spell at the start of the game. The more the game went on the more we were in command. We could have won more emphatically but really I'm delighted. This was the best team that Australia could put out – or so they were saying before the game – and we have had our problems with injuries and travel. As well as the win I'm just happy we got through with no more injuries turning up. That helps ...'

JUNE 9 – Another day, another flight. This time Rangers make the shorter hop from Sydney to Brisbane where the Scots are set to play another national select team. Before flying from Sydney Airport, though, there is ample evidence of the respect Rangers have won with their opening win. Approaches are made to Jock Wallace asking him if he would be interested in becoming Australia's national coach at a salary of £12 500 a year. Typically Wallace's answer is: 'There's only one team I want to manage – and that's the Rangers!'

As Wallace plays it cool, trying to assess his injuries and prepare for another tough game, Italian Tony Boggi enters the scene. Boggi is bossing the select team Rangers will meet and spends most of his time telling the Press exactly what his players are going to do to the Scots. While Boggi talks and talks Wallace ponders still, the possibility of a replacement player.

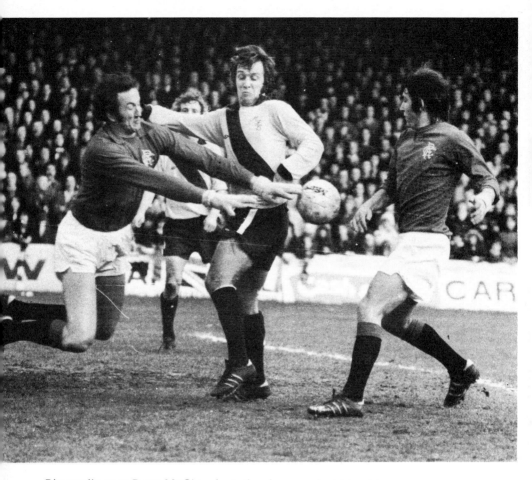

Big goalkeeper Peter McCloy, in action here against his old club Motherwell as he saves from Bobby Graham, took his chance on the world tour. With Stewart Kennedy late in arriving from the Scotland tour McCloy re-established himself as first choice keeper.

JUNE 10 – The injury call-over at the hotel shows Wallace that he has no alternative but to field the team which won in Sydney. Young Ally Dawson is suffering from a throat infection and Martin Henderson is the sole substitute. Really, the team selection is made for him . . .

He remains buoyant, though, and sends word to the fans back home: 'We are going for a repeat victory. That was a tremendous display and I was delighted that the two Scotland players arrived and went straight into action. Both Colin Jackson and Derek Parlane knew we needed them and they showed that they want to be successful on the tour. Bomber (Colin Jackson) was solid in

Colin Jackson missed the start of the tour because he was with
Scotland. Back home he missed few games in the season and here
he is tackling Motherwell and Scotland striker Willie Pettigrew.

defence and Derek's goals speak for themselves. These players
had to travel thousands of miles on their own to get here and join
us and that's the way they started – it's a tribute to them.

'We have difficulties with injuries but we have to get on with
it. There is nothing we can do about that. We had injuries for
the first game too, and we won it. All we want now is to do the
same again.'

JUNE 11 – Wallace's brave words can't disguise the Rangers'
problems and they lose 1–0 in the Brisbane Stadium. Australia
draw on all their resources and make changes from the side which
went down to Rangers in Sydney. The Scots, in contrast, limp
into the game with just twelve fit players. By half time they are

down to eleven fit men. Bobby McKean is taken ill during the first half and Martin Henderson, the only replacement available, goes on.

The Australians score in the first half in a breakaway attack and Rangers fight to try to get an equalizer. Losing McKean doesn't help them, and nor does an injury to skipper John Greig near the end. The odds against them have been too great.

Characteristically Jock Wallace refuses to hide behind excuses. He doesn't mention the cruel list of injuries after the game but says: 'The Australians played well. They were a better team than we were on the day. We are disappointed because we had set our hearts on going through the tour undefeated. Now that is not to be. What we have to do now is make it up to our fans in the next game. We have to play Victoria and we want to get back to our best in that one.'

JUNE 12 – Rangers move on to Melbourne, smarting from their first defeat and still hearing the voice of Tony Boggi telling them how they will plunge to a second defeat in this city. Boggi is in charge of the Australian team again. Still Jock Wallace refuses to get into a war of words. He says simply: 'There is no way we will lose two games in succession. Our lads have too much pride to allow another defeat to follow hard on the heels of that first one. We will be back on the winning trail against Victoria.'

The hotel resembles a scene from *General Hospital*. Ally Dawson and Bobby McKean are trying to shake off the effects of illness, John Greig, Tom Forsyth, Stewart Kennedy and Alex MacDonald are all receiving treatment for injuries. Wallace's words take on a brave new ring when you take a count and realize that the Rangers' boss is down to eleven fully fit players. By now too, a replacement has been ruled out. Too little time to make all the arrangements is the reason. Anyone joining the party would be with them for only the last two games.

JUNE 13 – A work out in Melbourne brings a gleam of hope for Wallace and his men. The injuries respond to treatment – being given almost non-stop by physiotherapist Tom Craig. The team boss is now hopeful that the only men missing from the game with Victoria will be Alex MacDonald and Stewart Kennedy. The other two injured players, Greig and Forsyth, train with the others while McKean and Dawson are fighting off the viruses which have struck them. Only one cloud remains for him – not the defeat, but the fact that he has not been able to experiment as much as he had hoped. 'I wanted to try things on this tour.' He maintains, 'that's what tours are for. There were ideas I had in mind that I wanted to use in competitive matches. Unfortunately there has been no way I could do this. OK, in one way, the injuries have forced me into using the youngsters Dawson and Henderson more than I might have. They have done well, both of them, but they were pushed into the side through necessity. That isn't the way I wanted to do things. I really looked on this as a chance to try out new formations, fresh approaches, different roles for certain players – and that hasn't been on.'

In spite of all that, Wallace remains happy that his players have responded so well to the challenges thrown up for them. The travel has been demanding, the heat and the playing surfaces sometimes against them, and the injury toll a never-ending burden. But the Scottish champions refuse to allow any of these problems to get them down. The 'character' which Wallace talks about so frequently has shone through yet again.

JUNE 14 – Tony Boggi and the Australian Press begin a propaganda blast which builds the pressure on Rangers. Rangers are being written off and while Wallace is angry he knows that he must answer the critics on the field of play.

It threatens to be another hard fixture. Two Scots-born players who were members of Australia's World Cup squad in the West German finals just a year earlier are in the Victoria team. They are goalkeeper Jack Reilly, once with Hibs, and midfield man Jim McKay. Victoria, bolstered by their coach's predictions expect to win.

JUNE 15 – With so much going against them Rangers rise to the challenge magnificently. They give their best performance of the tour as they rampage to a 5–1 victory over the Victoria Select team. And at last they silence the boastful Boggi!

This is a glory display from Rangers, the kind which helped them clinch their championship back home and the Australians are hammered to defeat. Angered by the pre-match forecasts of another defeat the Rangers' players react in the best possible way – they score three goals in the opening twenty minutes of the game. Derek Johnstone starts this dynamic spell with the first goal and Colin Stein and Bobby McKean follow up to shatter the Aussies. After half time Derek Parlane scores a fourth before Victoria get their only goal. Another of their World Cup squad members, Yugoslav striker Branco Buljevic gets their goal. Almost immediately, though, it is cancelled out.

Bobby McKean scores the fifth and Rangers win easily. In the end only heroics from Jack Reilly stop the Scots scoring an even more convincing win. Twice the ex-Easter Road man saves miraculously to stop Derek Johnstone getting a hat trick. It all goes right for Rangers at last. As well as the fine victory the injury situation eases enough to allow Wallace the luxury of using three substitutes. Martin Henderson goes on for Tommy McLean, Graham Fyfe for Colin Stein and Stewart Kennedy makes his first tour appearance when he allows Peter McCloy a rest for the final ten minutes.

All of which satisfies the Ibrox boss. But he gets as much pleasure at hearing Tony Boggi eat his words. The Italian admits: 'We were annihilated by the speed of Rangers. They destroyed us and we could not find any answer to them. Our players were not fit enough or fast enough. Rangers were very, very impressive.'

JUNE 16 – Another hop by plane – this time the shortest of the trip – and Rangers arrive at West Beach Airport in Adelaide. Here they have to prepare for a game against South Australia. Wallace is supremely confident after the performance against Victoria. He points out: 'We wanted to put the record straight for some of the critics in Australia. They haven't tried to understand the injury problems we have had. These have wrecked so much of our tactical planning on the tour. Anyhow, we did show them in Melbourne how we could play and we want to keep that up. If we do then I'm sure we will win comfortably. It was important in the last game that I was able, once again, to play Derek Johnstone in a forward position. That gave a fresh dimension to our attacking play . . .'

Tom Forsyth and Alex MacDonald are now the only casualties.

JUNE 17 – The tartan tinge which has been so evident on the tour, surfaces in Adelaide too. It's there among the fans who swarm around the hotel and also in the South Australian Soccer Federation itself. Their liaison officer who is in charge of welcoming Rangers and looking after them during their stay is Alex Hastings the one time Sunderland and Scotland wing half. He tells Rangers that they will face a huge crowd when they play the game at the Hindmarsh Stadium. He also warns Jock Wallace that South Australia have a fairly impressive record against touring teams. They drew 2–2 when Jackie Charlton's Middlesbrough team played in Adelaide and they beat the powerful Polish team, Legia of Warsaw, 2–1.

Almost coinciding with that news is a fresh injury worry. This time the player who hirples through a training session is Tommy McLean, so often a key man on the tour so far. Says Wallace: 'He

Derek Parlane, seen here in action against Ayr United defender Joe Fillippi, was a late arrival in Australia – but he started the tour in scoring style!

doesn't look too good but I want him fit for this game. I don't want to disturb the team who did so well against Victoria.'

JUNE 18 – Just as Alex Hastings forecasts Rangers take the field in front of thirty-three thousand fans. It's one of the biggest crowds the Australians have known and another tribute to the drawing power of the Scots. McLean is fit and Wallace is able to name an unchanged team which is: McCloy; Miller, Dawson; McKean, Jackson, Greig; McLean, Johnstone, Parlane, Young and Stein. It was good enough to thrash Victoria and it is good enough to win again – though the game is very much tighter!

South Australia are organized and determined and at half time the teams are still level at 0–0. Then in sixty-one minutes disaster strikes Rangers when skipper John Greig handles the ball in the penalty box and James Lean scores from the penalty kick for the Aussies. Now Rangers are down and they realize this is much more formidable than the five goal romp in Melbourne.

But Rangers draw on their reserves of character and just six minutes after the South Australia goal they are level once more. Bobby McKean crosses and Derek Parlane goes up to head the ball into the net. That sends the exiles in the huge crowd wild and they are celebrating again ten minutes from the end when the winner arrives. Parlane wins the ball in the air and sends it for goal where a defender stops it on the line with his hands. It's another penalty and Alex Miller comes up to score. Afterwards Wallace admits readily: 'We had it hard out there because South Australia are the best team we have played on the tour so far. It was a great, great game.'

That verdict was echoed by the fans who cheered the teams from the park at the end.

JUNE 19 – Now Rangers face the last game of their marathon tour but their preparations are hit from the beginning. Fog sweeps in and their flight to Perth is delayed for five hours. It is the kind of frustration Wallace wanted to avoid as he tries to keep his players for the game against Western Australia. He says: 'Hanging around airports is a killer for players. This is the type of thing which affects players' performances and we have lost vital time when we could have been treating the injuries which Tom Forsyth and Alex MacDonald are suffering from. There seems a chance that they will play in the last game but this flight problem could affect their fitness chances. And we want to win again to finish this tour in a bit of style . . .'

JUNE 20 – Rangers have an afternoon work out at the Perry Lake Stadium where they will play their last match. Earlier they had been relaxing in a bid to shake off the travel fatigue of the previous day. Forsyth and MacDonald are fit enough for training – but they remain doubtful for the game itself.

Wallace emphasizes: 'It will be good to have them back if they are 100 per cent ready to play – but we don't have to take chances. There is no need to do that – not now. We have had to survive the tour with more or less constant injury problems. They came at the very beginning so I think we can limp through the last game OK. We could have done without the injuries because they have added to the difficulties of the tour. Still, we didn't set out with the idea of having things easy. This was never meant to be a holiday trip.'

JUNE 21 – The injury jinx on tour is bad enough. Now, though, comes word from home that Sandy Jardine has been to see a specialist and may miss the start of the season. The news is black but Wallace does see some consolation in the shape of a tour bonus! 'If the news from home is correct and Sandy misses the kick off,' he reflects, 'then we have Ally Dawson ready to step in. This tour has proved that he can do a job in the first team. It's been lucky that he has had this opportunity and lucky, too, we were able to use him on this tour the way we did.'

Wallace decides to bring Stewart Kennedy back into the team. It is the first full game the keeper has been asked to play since the disaster at Wembley when England scored against him five times. He was an injury victim when he joined the party in Australia and ten minutes as substitute against Victoria is all the football he has played. Now his ankle injury has cleared and he gets his chance because Peter McCloy needs a break. McCloy has been asked to play non-stop through the tour.

JUNE 22 – The high hopes which Jock Wallace held of ending the tour with another victory disappear in the Perry Lake Stadium where ten thousand fans see the Scottish champions lose their second match in Australia. This time the Rangers team is: Kennedy; Miller, Dawson; McKean, Jackson, Greig; McLean, Johnstone, Parlane, Fyfe and Young.

Rangers look jaded and for almost the whole first half they are under pressure from the Australian team. Then minutes before half time comeback man Kennedy saves them. Western Australia are awarded a penalty and the tall 'keeper holds the shot. That seems to inspire Rangers and twin strikers Derek Parlane and Derek Johnstone combine to score the opening goal of the game. Parlane's power in the air sees him win the ball and head it down accurately to the unmarked Johnstone. He calmly slams the ball into the net from six yards' range. That gives Rangers a half time lead – but the Australians are determined that the Scots won't say in front. In seventy-six minutes their striker Ray Illiott levels the scores and minutes later Rangers are hit by a second blow when Derek Johnstone scores a second but sees it disallowed. Eight minutes from the end that decision becomes vital because Western Australia score the winner and Rangers' late attacks come too late to save the game. It is a day of disappointment . . .

John Greig, the iron-man skipper, left for the World tour after •
being plagued by injury. He returned to play with this kind of
determination in every one of Rangers' matches. Here he is
against Celtic and their young midfield man Jackie McNamara.

JUNE 23 – Jock Wallace relaxes in Perth and reflects on that
final match . . . and on the whole tour. The games are over, the
team is packing for the flight home and so it is a time to take
stock. He says: 'We should have had that last game won but we
missed chances and we lost it. It means that we have ended the
tour with a defeat – but that should not hide the value of the tour.

'This was a highly successful mission for Rangers. Injuries gave
us problems and prevented us trying out many things we had
planned.

'That meant, though, that we had to improvize a bit in certain
games because players weren't available. So we gained a bit from

that. Also we had players having to cope with different conditions from those at home. We played on larger pitches than there are at home and then there was the difference in climate. They had to deal with these changes and this helps when it comes to playing European ties. Let's face it, you don't get the same conditions in parts of the Continent as we have at home – the players have to adapt then and so they have learned to do it on tour.

'Naturally it would have been a great achievement to go home undefeated but that was asking a lot from the lads. They had the problems I've mentioned and they had a fair amount of travelling to do. That takes its toll. Still, I'm happy with what we have managed to do on this trip. We wanted to let our fans in exile see us play and we have done that. We wanted to foster team spirit for the challenges of next season at home – and we have done that too. That's what it's been about.'

And so the farewells are said at the hotel and at the airport where the usual band of Scots wait to see Rangers off on their long trek home. They leave behind many good memories and a powerful impression of the standards of Scottish football. They have won friends and they take home with them an increased admiration for the football they have seen in Australia. Wallace tells the Australians: 'The success you had in 1974 when the Australian national team qualified for the World Cup Finals in West Germany has given the game a shot in the arm here. We know what it did for us in Scotland. It rekindled interest and had the whole country thinking about the team . . .

'That's why I can imagine how it was here in Australia, a country where you are still fighting to establish soccer.

'Everyone in Australia must have sat up to take notice of the team because here it was taking on the best countries in the world. The best team we played against wasn't, funnily enough, one of the teams which beat us. Most of the players agree with me on this. In our view the best team we faced was South Australia. They had organization and skill and we just managed to beat them. It was the best game we played on the whole tour . . .'

JUNE 24 – The tour is behind them. Rangers are home again, travel stained and weary after flying from the other side of the world. Ally Dawson who left Scotland twenty-seven days earlier as an unknown returns now to find fans looking for his autograph at Glasgow Airport. In Wallace's words seventeen-year-old Dawson 'left as a boy and he has come home as a man!'

It's over at last, the longest tour in Ibrox history, one which carried them around the world and renewed the faith of so many of their faraway supporters.

A LITTLE BIT OF BLARNEY IN EUROPE

Rangers' success in winning the Scottish championship meant more than adding another of soccer's top prizes to their already laden honours list.

It meant, of course, that they had broken the ten-years-long stranglehold that Old Firm rivals Celtic had had on the Scottish League title. And it meant, too, that the Ibrox team were back playing in the European Cup after eleven long years out of the tournament of champions.

The fans looked forward to Europe. They began to talk about the teams which might arrive at Ibrox when the draw was made. They dreamed of the holders, Bayern Munich, old foes of Rangers, or the West German champions Borussia Moenchengladbach, another team Rangers had played, of Benfica and Real Madrid and Dynamo Kiev or Derby County. Name after glittering name tripped off the tongues of the Ibrox fans at the start of July when the draw for the European competitions was made in Zürich.

And, at the end of it all, Rangers were paired off with Bohemians of Dublin. Sure, they were the Irish champions, but there was no way the Rangers' fans could work up any enthusiasm for THAT first round draw! Even at Ibrox on the day the draw was made the most that a club spokesman could comment was – 'Well, we won't have any travel problems . . .'

Then Manager Jock Wallace began to study the fixture. He decided that he could take no chances – though he knew that it was the kind of simple stepping-stone back to the big time that his team needed.

And amidst a blast of blarney from the other side of the Irish Sea, Wallace went to work methodically. He saw Bohemians play Hibs in a pre-season Dublin challenge game when they pushed the Easter Road men enough to be beaten by a single goal – that, at a time when their team was weakened.

He also planned to watch them later to assess them under competitive conditions. Nothing would be left to chance.

Little Tommy McLean, picked out as the danger man for
Rangers by Bohemians' Manager Billy Young, seen here scoring
a goal against Hibs at Ibrox. The Hibs' players are goalkeeper
Jim McArthur and centre half Roy Barry – McLean missed the
first Bohemians' match.

Wallace went about his work quietly. In Dublin, though, it
was all a bit different. Report after report reached Glasgow.
Some said Rangers were not welcome because their fans would
make trouble . . . others said they would be given the kind of
welcome reserved for top class European teams.

Then, finally, came the real piece of Bohemians' blarney – a
plea to change the venues of the two-legged tie. Their team

manager Billy Young said: 'We don't want to play the first leg of the tie at Ibrox – we would prefer it at Dalymount. It would mean a bigger crowd for us because we won't get so many if we lose a few goals at Ibrox, now will we?'

Rangers, though, would not budge. They knew that Bohemians had built a reputation for a tough and organised defence And they remembered that Dalymount had been a graveyard for many international teams before Rangers . . .

They wanted to win and going to Dalymount first was not the best way to achieve their objective. At Ibrox they firmly told the Irish that they would stand by the draw as made by the European Union.

And so the pre-match skirmishing went on. Jock Wallace went to Dalymount once again, saw Bohemians draw 0–0 with Athlone and warned: 'Bohemians are a well organized team. They are competent in defence and it will be hard to get goals against them . . .'

Billy Young travelled to Ibrox and saw Rangers struggle against a defensively-minded St Johnstone. His verdict? 'Now Rangers are a good team,' he told waiting pressmen after the game, 'but there were a few times they struggled today. I'll take a tip or two from St Johnstone. We'll probably drop into a 4–4–2 set up right at the start and let them have a go at us.

'We can push the ball about a bit better than St Johnstone. We will use possession football as much as we can to frustrate Rangers. Their main danger man is the little man, Tommy McLean and I'm sure we can keep the ball away from him.'

That was a job which Young and his players didn't have to do . . . for McLean failed a fitness test before that first leg tie in September. And on a night of teeming rain Tom Forsyth, Sandy Jardine and Alex MacDonald were also missing. Forsyth and Jardine were injured – but MacDonald later became the subject of a Rangers protest to the European Union. They had been informed that the player was banned from the match because of a caution picked up two years earlier. Only later – after the game – did the European Union admit to a clerical error. That was too late to help Rangers in a worrying pre-match time . . .

But the worries Wallace had disappeared inside an hour of the match against the Irishmen. And the man who did most

McLean's midfield partner, Alex MacDonald, was also ruled out of the Bohemians' game – by a wrong ruling from the European Union. He later became the subject of a Rangers' protest to the Continental bosses – but here Celtic's Danny McGrain looks as if he wishes the ban was for domestic games. MacDonald is in full flight as he carries the ball clear of the Scotland right back.

to chase his problems away was Graham Fyfe, playing only his second game of the season. Fyfe scored the first goal and made two others in a 4–1 win which turned the return game in Dublin into a formality.

Fyfe was the darling of the 24 000 fans that night. He scored easily after twenty minutes and even though Terry Flanagan equalized in thirty-seven minutes, Rangers were back in front two minutes later. Colin Stein harried centre half Joe Burke into an own goal mistake which sent Rangers in with a half-time lead. Fyfe then stepped in twice in the second half to start moves which gave the remaining goals to Alex O'Hara and Derek Johnstone. Wallace was delighted after the game. He had wanted the tie sewn up at Ibrox, wanted to go to Dublin with a big lead to cushion his side for the second leg challenge. And, in spite of the team problems, the players had succeeded in giving him that.

Naturally Bohemians' boss Billy Young made as much as he could of scoring an away goal which could count double. And he added: 'We were a bit unlucky with one or two of the Rangers' goals. If we have their luck at Dalymount then we're still in there with a chance!'

The blarney, though, was now wearing out. Even Bohemians didn't really believe they had a chance – and the only Rangers' worries when they travelled to Dublin came from IRA threats and travel problems!

The problems with travel, something they had expected to be trouble-free, occurred because of an industrial dispute at Glasgow. The team had to leave from Edinburgh a little earlier than they had planned . . .

That was easily solved. The threats which came their way were more worrying . . . especially as general manager Willie Waddell had made strong efforts to avoid trouble during the club's return to Europe. He had made an appearance before the first leg match at Ibrox asking the fans to behave. They had done so . . .

Then, when tickets for the return game went on sale, Rangers insisted on taking the names and addresses of all purchasers so that any trouble makers might be more easily traced.

But, suddenly, the threats to the team's safety arrived. Rangers had taken the precaution of staying outside Dublin and while Bohemians made a great play of security arrangements at the Dalymount Stadium the Scots knew that very few of their fans were going to 'follow, follow' to Dublin for a match which was a mere formality.

Striker Colin Stein dropped out of the first team later in the season – but he did score to help Rangers to their 4–1 European Cup victory over Bohemians of Dublin at Ibrox.

As they made their final preparations for the match itself the IRA threats arrived at various newspaper offices. The Rangers' party were warned that they should travel to the game at Dalymount by 'armoured car'. The threats, though, were kept from the players who trained in the quiet seclusion of a hotel at the seaside village of Killiney outside Dublin. The relaxed and confident team met with no trouble until after the game – and by that time they were through to the second round of the European Cup.

Wallace maintained before the game that he wanted to win the second leg tie – and he believed that he could do it with the team he selected. Graham Fyfe was in again, looking for goals, and young Ally Dawson made his European debut. The team was: McCloy; Miller, Dawson; Greig, Jackson, Young; McLean, MacDonald, Parlane, Johnstone and Fyfe. It had a balanced and experienced look about it even though Sandy Jardine and Tom

Graham Fyfe, on the right of the picture, is now with Hibs. Here, though, he was warming up for a European Cup game. He comes in to assist Sandy Jardine after Hertha Berlin skipper Erich Beer moves clear of the Rangers' tackle. Fyfe went on to be the star of the first game with Bohemians of Dublin at Ibrox. He scored one goal and made two more. Then, at the end of the season, he moved to Hibs.

Forsyth were still missing. Wallace's hopes of a second victory, though, did not happen. That was just beyond a Rangers' team who dominated most of the game but were defied by Bohemians' goalkeeper Joe Smyth.

Derek Johnstone guided a header into the net after a John Greig free kick seven minutes before half-time and that was good enough for an interval lead. Mind you, Smyth had saves from Cutty Young, John Greig and Tommy McLean before that goal, which had Jock Wallace, an ex-keeper himself enthusing over his performance after the game. In fifty-six minutes Turlough O'Conner equalized to save some of the Irish honour and the tiny crowd – small because the Rangers' fans had not travelled and the Dubliners knew their team had no chance – cheered them from the field. Certainly they had played better than they had done at Ibrox. Their defence had stood firm and O'Conner had caused Rangers some moments of trouble in attack.

But, of course, everyone who knew the European scene had realized that the job had been done at Ibrox. Rangers went to Dalymount in the knowledge that they would not be knocked out of Europe in the first round.

Their thoughts had been on the second round draw just as much as on the return game with the Irish part-timers.

Still, their joy was scarred on the way back to their hotel, when the threatened trouble exploded in one incident as the team bus with its police escort was making its way down O'Connell Street. A bottle was hurled through the bus window, shattering it and striking team boss Jock Wallace on the face. It was a frightening moment as the bus driver and the police motor cycle outriders put on speed to get away from the scene as quickly as possible. The team were still shaken when they reached their hotel but, fortunately, boss Wallace was only slightly cut around his eye. It was a sad end to the trip which had gone so much Rangers' way . . .

It curbed any celebrations the team had planned and flying home the next day all the talk centred on the draw which was to be made twenty-four hours later. Wallace admitted that he hoped for a reasonably easy second round tie – allowing the team to build gradually to the quarter finals and the Continent's big guns.

It was not to be, however. Instead of a pairing with a Scandinavian club – the exact type of tie he would have liked – Wallace, instead, found Rangers drawn to meet the formidable French champions St Etienne. They had been beaten semi-finalists the previous season, losing to the evenutal European Cup winners, Bayern Munich. Now Rangers had to face them. . . .

THE ART OF STRIKING
by Derek Parlane and Martin Henderson

One of the more intriguing challenges set up during Rangers' chase for the Scottish 'Treble' last season was that between two of their strikers ...

On one hand was Derek Parlane, a Scottish international, a recognized first team man for several seasons, and an outstanding leader of any forward line ...

On the other was nineteen-year-old Martin Henderson, 'discovered' as a first team player on the world tour in the close-season and then the man in possession for a great part of the year.

The fans were split ... should Parlane, their hero for so long, be in the team or should Henderson, in goal scoring form, hold onto that place? It was a problem for Manager Jock Wallace, too, although a happy one in many ways. After all, no one else in Scotland had two such dangerous strikers to juggle with. As Wallace pointed out: 'Rangers must be the envy of every club in the country because we are able to have a player of Derek Parlane's ability on the substitute bench for a long spell.'

Anyhow, the two strikers were rarely out of the news and figured constantly in the terracing arguments. That's why I went to them – to the men the fans were talking about so much – to find out their views on that so delicate art of striking. It is one of the most important and so often one of the most elusive soccer arts of all. In this chapter it is examined by two of the best exponents in Scottish soccer ...

GALLACHER – First of all I'd like to ask you what you think are the most important attributes for a striker in the modern game?

PARLANE – I don't think that there is any doubt about it – you must train yourself to be very, very sharp inside the penalty area.

Derek Parlane raises his hand in salute after scoring against Hibs in his comeback game after injury. Rangers went on to win 2–0.

To make sure that you are you have to work very hard at being fast off your mark. This is vitally important. Also, when I say sharpness I don't just mean speed in reaching a ball, I mean that you have to be able to get shots in at goal without hesitation. There just isn't the time available to tee a ball up and make certain before shooting. You have to be prepared to hit shots immediately you see an opening . . .

HENDERSON – Well, I'd go along with what Derek says of course. But I'd add courage. I think that players have to be brave if they are playing in the opposition penalty area for most of a game. Then, as Derek says, the ability to snatch a half chance and good positioning in the box. This takes experience, naturally, and lots of confidence. Willie Pettigrew of Motherwell showed last season how much confidence was an ingredient. When he was sticking his goals away he did it without thinking – it was as if he KNEW he was going to score whenever he hit the ball. There was never a sign of nerves, never a moment of indecision – that's important.

GALLACHER – You talked about speed off the mark without elaborating on it. How do you achieve this exactly?

PARLANE – Hard work! Really, that's the answer, it's a long hard slog, getting out on the track with spikes on and working on sprint after sprint always of varying distances. The Boss (Manager Jock Wallace) often works it out for you. He has you doing sprints over fifteen yards, then twenty yards and then up to thirty yards – not very often much more than that.

These sprints are designed to have you moving quickly from a standing start over a short distance. They try to achieve the kind of situation you may come up against in the box during a game. You don't have to run a hundred yards then – it's a short, sharp dash and these sprints help you in that.

HENDERSON – Actually when I first went to Ibrox as a boy we had a special running coach, Tom Paterson, who died a short time ago. He took a lot of time guiding young players in how to run properly. He helped me enormously when I first came to the club. Like Derek says, you had short sprints gradually building up to longer sprints and Tom used to have the stop watch on you to let you know how your times were comparing as you worked. He used to keep us at it, working tremendously hard with the emphasis on these short sprints. He paid great attention to detail. I used to run with my arms swinging all wrong and he kept at me until I had them swinging properly and this helped my pace. That may sound silly – but the little things all

Here's nineteen years old Martin Henderson scoring against two of the players he respects most in the Premier League. It's at Ibrox against Ayr United and the defenders are Rikki Fleming (right) and Alex McAnespie just behind the young striker.

add up. I know how much faster I became because he was ready to point out the little things to me. They helped you shave seconds off your times and that's what Tom was always after. He was so good that at one time he had Sandy Jardine entering for professional sprints at athletics meetings. I suppose it was typical of the whole set-up at Ibrox. The tiniest detail is looked after, every little thing which will help make you a better player. I know how important it all was for me.

GALLACHER – Now let's talk about the courage Martin mentioned earlier. I remember once Hugh Curran, who was with Wolves at the time, being picked for Scotland and he told me there was no place for cowards in the penalty box. What exactly does all this talk mean?

PARLANE – Well, you just have to be prepared to take a lot

of knocks. It all boils down to that. You get whacked by defenders and you have to take it and get on with the game.

Strikers have the ball played forward to them and very often have to collect it with their backs to the opposing goal – and to the opposing defenders. That's when you get hit and hit hard. But there is no use looking over your shoulder and worrying about it. You have to concentrate on gathering the ball or playing it off to one of your own players. Sometimes you just don't know what's going to hit you but you can't let it bother you. If you start worrying then you lose concentration and your game will suffer.

HENDERSON – That sums it up. You don't know what's behind you. And you can't let yourself worry about it. You have to shield the ball as it reaches you no matter if you are going to

Derek Parlane is in the dark blue jersey of Scotland here as he scores against Northern Ireland and Spurs' hero Pat Jennings in a Hampden international. Now Parlane is after his Scotland place once more . . .

get hammered in the back or not. OK, you get a few knocks that way but you have to take them. Again, you can't allow yourself to be intimidated. When you first come into the team as I did last season then you get older players trying to talk you off your game and trying to make you nervous and uncertain. You have got to ignore them and just play away. If you show some hard man defender that you are worrying about him you might as well walk off the field. You have to stand up for yourself a bit . . .

GALLACHER – When British teams first moved into European football – long before either of your times – they used to be criticized for stereo-typed attacking. High balls into the penalty area for a burly striker used to be the main weapon and this was supposed to be the wrong way to go about things. Now it seems to be on the way back – and it seems to be working against the Continental defences. They never look too comfortable against strikers who are good in the air. Would you agree with that? Is power in the air a very vital asset to any team and any striker?

PARLANE – I've got to think so, haven't I? Really, though, you don't get too many small strikers going about nowadays. It's another part of your game you have to work at, of course. Nothing comes easy. I think that Joe Jordan is one of the best players in the air anywhere in the world. He gets up well and when he is playing with Leeds he's knocking the ball down to Alan Clarke or whoever may be playing alongside him. And the Continentals don't like it all that much.

When you practise this you have to have some of the lads hitting balls into you from various angles. Then you have to get up for them and this helps in timing your jump and in accuracy when you make contact. I suppose anyone watching would think it's monotonous but it is to strengthen your neck muscles. It's important to have power behind your headers and strong neck muscles can give you this. I used to go back in the afternoons for this kind of thing and the Boss and Tommy Craig, the physiotherapist, used to help me a lot. They would spend time with me when I went back for extra training.

HENDERSON – This is something I'm still working on in my own game. I know I could be better than I am at the present. Really I would like to be as good as Derek Johnstone is. He really climbs to some height and then he hangs there to get his header in. After playing for a while in the Premier League now I think it's more important than ever to be strong in the air. As far as I can see at the moment a lot of the centre halves in Scotland are not as clever as they might be. Rikki Fleming and Alex

Both the Rangers' strikers are in this one — the opponents are Ayr United at Somerset Park and Henderson watches as Parlane blasts a shot against Ayr defender Billy Paton while Dave McCulloch looks on.

McAnespie of Ayr United are the two defenders I rate highest of the ones I've played against. They are first and then Willie McVie of Motherwell is good too – especially when the ball is coming straight towards him.

GALLACHER – OK, you've both answered that one pretty emphatically. Now what influences have there been on your own personal approaches to striking? Are there any particular players you have tried to copy? Or anyone who has given you advice which has helped you form your own particular style?

PARLANE – When I first started out as a striker the man I used to admire most was Martin Chivers of Spurs and England. He had this tremendous natural strength and the ability to hold defenders off as he gathered a ball. He was the perfect target man for any team because he had these physical attributes going for him. That was early on in my own career, though, and I don't really think that I model myself on any one player at all. At least I don't do it consciously. But I do find myself watching strikers almost exclusively when I am at some games as a spectator. They are the men who matter to me and so even when the ball might not be with them or even in their direction I'm looking at them closely to see how they position themselves. I watch to see how they try to lose the men marking them, what runs they might try to get space for themselves, things like that. I suppose in that way I'm picking up a little hint here and another there and it probably goes into use in my own game.

Among the players I admire are Alan Clarke because he teams up so well with Joe Jordan at Leeds just as he used to team up with Mick Jones a few seasons back. He can be tremendously sharp in the box and he is the type of player who hits the ball as soon as it reaches him. He doesn't try to delay as he sizes up a chance – he lets go whenever he has a glimpse of the goal. Also nowadays I love watching John Toshack and Kevin Keegan of Liverpool on the telly. They work so well together that they are a lesson to many of us.

I don't think it would be too much of an exaggeration to say that most of Liverpool's recent successes have come through this pair. Their understanding on the field is almost telepathic. It's uncanny the way that they play those little one-two moves which just open up defences. Funnily enough I never used to rate Toshack very highly when he was playing for Wales and I was in the Scotland squad. That's going back a few years. Now he has blossomed with his country and his club and playing the way he is right now he will give us problems in the World Cup qualifying games when they come round. I mean, let's face it – he's even getting goals with his feet now!

HENDERSON – Well, I don't want to get Derek blushing but he is one player I have watched and tried to emulate. The other one is Derek Johnstone. I know they both play for Rangers – but I'm not being influenced by that at all. They are the two players I have tried to learn from. Both of them shield the ball well and this is one of those important assets we were talking about earlier on. Derek Johnstone, of course, has picked up so much experience in a lot of different positions. He has been an out and out striker, a centre half, a sweeper, a midfield man – he's done just about everything and done it all so well. He is the most complete player I know.

And the other Derek, well, he had a midfield spell too to widen his experience. When I was a reserve I used to love being able to watch them in action. And then when I was named as substitute quite a few times back at the start of the season I saw them often at close range. That was an education for me. It was great just to sit back and drink it all in.

As I have said elsewhere Derek Johnstone is just about unbeatable in the air but Derek Parlane has other things going for him too. He gets up OK and guides his headers well and while people always seem to talk about his strength and his running power they should never overlook his skill. He is a very skilful player.

He has helped a lot by telling me what runs I should be making and he just never seems to stop moving himself. He makes a tremendous contribution to the team. When I've played alongside him he has been telling me to keep going, try running across each other, moving about the whole time to confuse the men who are marking us. I've seen myself finish up exhausted and Derek is still going powerfully. He is a wonderful example to any young player. Another player I've admired in the Premier League is Bobby Graham of Motherwell. He has impressed me even more than his team-mate Willie Pettigrew. I know Willie has scored all the goals but Bobby has so much experience and craft. We have usually had to get Tom Forsyth to mark him very tightly when we have met Motherwell. Obviously he picked up many little things when he was down south, first with Liverpool and then with Coventry, and he draws on all that experience now. Again he is such a skilful player.

GALLACHER – One of the great problems for any striker is when goals just seem to dry up. Often there is no apparent reason for this but it seems to hit everyone at some time or another.

Players just seem to go off the boil. How does it feel personally when this goal famine hits you? And is there any real remedy?

PARLANE – I've suffered from this quite a few times and it's terrible. It is quite the worst thing that can happen to any striker. The baffling thing is that you can still be playing OK,. even playing well, but you are not fulfilling your main function.

That is, after all, getting goals and when you start missing them then you are bound to worry. It does happen to everyone just like you said. Look at Bob Latchford of Everton last season, the most expensive striker in British football, and yet he wasn't getting goals. It just dries up. We all know that we can't score a goal every week or in every game – but when a thing like this hits you it seems to go on for week after week after week. I had it last season and I've had it before. Sometimes it vanishes as suddenly as it arrived. But while it is affecting you it really gets you down. When it happened to me for a spell last season I tried not to worry about it, not to get depressed – but it was impossible. It gets on top of you a bit.

There isn't any real answer. You simply have to keep working away at your game and sooner or later the goals will come back. You have to try extra shooting practice, extra heading practice, and then one day in one game you get a breakthrough and sometimes that's all you need. While it lasts, though, it's murder!

HENDERSON – The worst spell I had was when I was in the reserves and there wasn't so much pressure on me there. You can allow yourself a little more time to get over it when you are in the second team. When you are in the League side, though, that time isn't available. Often enough you can be hitting the ball well but goalkeepers are making great saves, or your tries are being deflected off target, or you are hitting the posts or the bar and you begin to feel that you are jinxed. When I moved into the first team I realized the kind of pressure that strikers can be under. I felt it then. I mean, there I was keeping a top player out of the side.

Derek Parlane was sitting on the bench and I knew I had to keep getting the ball in the net to keep my place in the team. Like Derek says, mind you, there is no easy way out of the rut once this lack of goals hits you. The main thing is to try not to allow it to affect your self-confidence. Once you lose confidence then it gets worse. At Ibrox, though, there are always people around willing to work with you and encourage you while you are going through a bad spell. That helps a whole lot.

GALLACHER – We've talked about strikers you admire and

The next two pictures show Martin Henderson's ability to shield the ball. This is one of the teenager's qualities pointed out by fellow goal scorer Derek Parlane.
(a) Henderson leans over to make it hard for Aberdeen international sweeper Willie Miller to get in his tackle.
(b) Another duel with Willie Miller and this time the Aberdeen sweeper can't get near the ball as the young Ibrox man brings it under control.

people who might have helped you in one way or another. Are there players you have to face whom you admire particularly. Or, to put it another way, are there players you just wouldn't want to have to face up to every week?

PARLANE – The most impressive man I have played against was Barry Hulshoff who was the stopper for Ajax and for Holland. He was the big fellow with the beard and when we met Ajax in a challenge game he was tremendous. It was a big double header prestige match between the holders of the European Cup, Ajax, and ourselves who were holders of the European Cup Winners Cup. We played them at Ibrox and at Amsterdam. And Hulshoff didn't give me too many chances to do anything. He was big, he was strong and he was fast . . . he has everything that you don't want to find in the guy who is playing against you. Then playing alongside him was a 'sweeper' from West Germany Horst Blankenberg. I think he is back in West Germany now playing with Hamburg. He was good too. In fact, they were just terrible to play against. I found it very, very difficult – if not completely impossible. They marked tight and that's always a problem to a striker and I just didn't seem able to get away from them. They were a formidable pair.

Then there is another player, and he isn't so well known – Chris Nicholl of Aston Villa and Ireland. I came up against him when he was playing for Northern Ireland against Scotland and I was in the Scots team. I don't think I won a ball against him in the air the entire night. Every ball in the air was his. He climbed so high and his timing was great. He was something else. He impressed me a lot and he isn't a player who is so very well known.

HENDERSON – I haven't had nearly as much experience as Derek, of course but I find it interesting that he should mention a couple of Continental players – because it's the same with me. The two men who played at the back, in the middle of the defence, that is, for St Etienne of France in the European Cup tie against us were different class. The most impressive of the two was the Argentinian Osvaldo Piazza. I was only on as a substitute for about twenty-five minutes or so and I found out how much experience I lacked when I came up against him. He seemed to know so much about the game and he was very, very strong. It wasn't that he was quick – it was just that he seemed able to read what you were thinking and he was with you all the time. And he seemed to stay fresh, fresher than me at the end of the game, even though I'd come on late. He knew what it was all about and I learned a lot about defenders from him that night. I'll never forget him because that was my first taste of a really class opponent.

GALLACHER – There was a great uproar down south last season when Tommy Docherty brought back wingers with Manchester United. He was using Steve Coppell and Gordon Hill and nothing like that had been done there since before Sir Alf Ramsey's wingless times.

Now Rangers use wingers too, they like players going wide down the flanks and it seems to be better for strikers to get their service from this area. Do you find it that way?

PARLANE – Very much because wingers can get round behind defences and then cut the ball back to their strikers. Everyone prefers to get balls played back to them in this way. Cutty Young did it for us when he first came back from Coventry. I used to love the way he got the ball over into the middle so quickly once he got past the full back. I love playing with wingers. Of course, we are especially lucky at Ibrox having a player like wee Tommy McLean around. Wee Tam was being used a lot going down the left wing last year and there is just no one who can pinpoint a cross more accurately than he does it. He has this knack of being able to find you as you move into position for a cross ball. And at free kicks he is just unbelievable. He is a superb dead ball, kicker and, again, he does it with this accuracy that no one else can match.

GALLACHER – Tommy Docherty once tried to buy Tommy McLean. That was when Tommy McLean was with Kilmarnock and the Doc was at Chelsea. And he wanted him just for this accuracy that you are talking about. He wanted wee Tam to land the ball right on Tony Hateley's head.

PARLANE – I'm glad he didn't get him and that Tommy came here – but certainly no one could have done that job better.

HENDERSON – I'd go along with that. I think he must be the most accurate passer of a ball in Britain. He flights it so perfectly and he makes it easy for us in the middle. Bobby McKean, the other winger, is slightly different, he gets the ball over well too but he chips it rather than flighting it the way the wee man does. Mind you both of them have helped me get goals and I think it's great to have wingers making ground down the flanks and getting that ball over.

GALLACHER – What ambitions do you have left in the game?

PARLANE – Well, I've been lucky enough to win a few honours with the club but I'd really like to win a European medal with Rangers. I played in the semi final of the European Cup Winners Cup the year we won it by beating Moscow Dynamo in the Barcelona final. But I was in as a replacement for John Greig who was injured. And so I was out again for the final and didn't get a medal. I'd like to make up for that some time in the future. I believe I will because the team is capable of winning the European Cup. That apart, I'd like to get my game together again, start getting goals and get into the Scotland squad in time for the World Cup games. I would really like to go with the team to Argentina for the 1978 Finals if we qualify.

HENDERSON – Mainly all I want to do is keep playing OK in the first team – and, in fact, just stay in the team. It would be great to get some recognition from Scotland later on but just now all I want is to do well at Ibrox. I have to concentrate on staying in the first team. That is a big enough challenge for me. There are older players and younger players challenging me and if I can establish myself then I'll be happy.

GALLACHER – Finally, Derek, a question for you alone. Martin has said how much he learned about the game, about striking, from watching you. Now that you have had a chance of seeing him in action in the first team how does he shape up?

PARLANE – Very well indeed. He shields the ball particularly well, and he keeps on the move all the time. By that I mean that he doesn't give opposing defenders the chance to rest, the chance of a breather if you like, while the game is going on. He is constantly harrying them, always in with a challenge. They don't get time to make good clean clearances because he is after them forcing them into mistakes.

Also he hits shots first time – exactly the way it should be done. Occasionally he uses his arms too much and gives away daft fouls – otherwise he has looked great. I've enjoyed playing with him, too, on the occasions we have been together. We worked OK, making diagonal runs to worry defenders and shouting well for cross balls. We had it together so that we wouldn't be going for the same crosses. One would be at one post, one at the other and whoever won it in the air would know that the other was ready for a knock back if that was on. It was fine and Martin progressed tremendously fast. Remember it was only on the close-season tour that he really was given his opportunity.

Parlane's tribute to the youngster who kept him out of the team for so long last season was spontaneous. Just as was Henderson's tribute to his experienced rival. All of this smacked of the comradeship Manager Jock Wallace stresses so much when he talks of his players at Ibrox. No complaints, no moans, just a feeling of playing for each other – and, more, playing for Rangers!

It's Derek Parlane with Scotland once more – during the Wembley disaster! Here the Rangers' star is outjumped by England centre half Dave Watson. Ted MacDougall is the other Scots' attacker with Kevin Beattie the England defender on the left.

FAILURE IN FRANCE!

The stars, the world class stars of soccer eluded Rangers once again when the draw for the European Cup second round was made.

There were no Beckenbauers, no Netzers, no Blochins, no Breitners when the team to face Rangers came out of the silver champagne bucket in Switzerland. Instead the Scottish champions found themselves drawn against the formidable French side, St Etienne. A team with no big names, a team lacking in the kind of glamour which surrounds Bayern Munich or Real Madrid . . . but a team carefully built to function as a unit.

St Etienne, runaway winners of the French title, were no Real Madrid – but nor were they another Bohemians. This was a team with a long European history, one which had pushed Old Firm rivals Celtic desperately close in a previous European Cup battle. That was in 1968 when Celtic lost 2–0 in France and then managed to win 4–0 at Celtic Park to carry them into the next round. . . .

But it had been dreadfully close and the current St Etienne coach Robert Herbin knew all about it. At that time the flame-haired Herbin had been the midfield powerhouse and inspiration for the French. Now he was their team boss.

And he still held memories of the game against Celtic when St Etienne complained bitterly about the refereeing. He wanted revenge and he wanted to take it against Rangers. Whenever the draw was made Herbin announced: 'We know about Scottish football. It is strong. It is fast – but it is not clever. Certainly Rangers have a long and proud reputation in Europe but we have no reason to fear them. I am happy that we shall be playing them. It is better this game than, perhaps, having to face Real Madrid or Bayern Munich or the Russians, Dynamo Kiev.'

Herbin's optimism seemed a little ill-placed when you considered his team's League position at the time he talked. They had dropped into sixth place and were eight points behind the League leaders Nice.

But the St Etienne manager based his views on his team's European experience – and their near success the season before. They reached the last four of the top Continental tournament then lost out to the eventual winners Bayern Munich 2–0 – both goals being scored in the Olympic Stadium in Munich after a draw in France. It is always an impressive statistic when a team can boast of reaching a European Cup semi-final. It is even more impressive when the teams beaten on the way there are sides with reputations of their own. Ibrox boss Jock Wallace looked back his records and found that Sporting Lisbon of Portugal, Hajduk Split of Yugoslavia and the dour Ruch Chorzow of Poland had fallen to the French before the Bayern clash.

The battle honours were the kind which any side in Europe would have been proud of.

These victories, too, told their own background story. St Etienne were a team who prepared as thoroughly as any team in Europe for these games. They used as their soccer spy Pierre Garronnaire, the club's technical director, and a man whose name was known across the Continent. Garronnaire came to Glasgow to put Rangers under the microscope . . . a French TV team came with him to film their games immediately before the first leg was due in France. Nothing was left to chance.

St Etienne team manager Robert Herbin watches Rangers crash by three goals to Ayr United at Somerset Park as he spies for the European Cup clash. Herbin is on the left in front – behind him is a grim looking Willie Waddell.

Rangers are in trouble in this picture from the second leg at
Ibrox. Goalkeeper Stewart Kennedy and right back Sandy Jardine
are both under pressure as Christian Synaeghel of St Etienne moves
in.

Meanwhile Wallace prepared, too. As always he did it without
publicity. There was none of the ballyhoo which surrounded the
French telly invasion of Ibrox. Instead he went quietly to see St
Etienne play in a League game at Nantes where they drew 2–2.
And while Garronnaire worried over Tommy McLean and Derek
Johnstone, Wallace planned to stop the French wingers Pierre
Rocheteau and Patrick Revelli. They were the men who impressed him most and they were also the men named as dangers
in a dossier Leeds United had had prepared the year before.
Their 'spy' Tony Collins had watched them just in case they were
the team to meet Leeds in that Paris final. Jock Wallace had
combed his files for a Bayern breakdown to give Leeds pre-match
aid and now Collins talked to Wallace about St Etienne.

But all the preparations in the world could not help Rangers
overcome two deadly blows which hit them in the Geoffrey
Guichard Stadium that October night . . .

That story, though, comes a little later. The week of the game was a vital one for Rangers and Jock Wallace. They had to face St Etienne on the Wednesday and then return to play Celtic in the League Cup Final at Hampden.

That early in the season, too, the injury toll had been heavy. Before flying out to France two days before the game Wallace growled: 'I have never been able to field the team I wanted this season. There has always been someone injured. Because of that we have not been able to find the rhythm we had going last season. We are taking longer to settle . . .

'Because of that we will be going to France drumming it into the players that they must have patience. This is the quality which can carry us through to the next round. Patience in these games away from home is essential. We can sit back a bit and draw them out. It has to be played that way. They are a good side and they use their wingers so well.

'I have checked the measurements of their ground and it must be one of the widest pitches in Europe. It is eighty-five yards wide

It's Stewart Kennedy and Sandy Jardine in bother again as two French forwards lurk waiting for a mistake. Kennedy, though, gathers the ball with Dominique Rocheteau the menacing man from St Etienne.

Here is one of the many aerial attacks which failed at Ibrox in the
European Cup second leg clash with St Etienne. The French
team's Yugoslav goalkeeper Ivan Curkovic rises to punch the
ball away from Rangers' attackers Colin Stein and Derek
Johnstone. The other St Etienne player is defender Gerard
Farison.

– and that's fifteen yards wider than Ibrox. This must encourage
them to use their wingers. They have the width – and they have
the men who use that width. Rocheteau and Revelli are old
fashioned wingers. It's a change to see that in Europe but there
it is – and I know how dangerous they will be.'

Wallace elected to play defensively. He wanted a 4–4–2 set up,
one which would be able to stop French attacks and then worry
them in counter-raids using Colin Stein and Derek Parlane up
front.

The French, naturally, looked for all out attack hoping that
the 'hard man' centre half from Argentina Osvaldo Piazza could
control the Rangers' strikers.

It seemed a fascinating clash. Both teams had done their home-work. Both teams would call on all their experience and skills.

There was a hint of possible greatness about the tie until the first of the two deadly blows which struck Rangers that night. This one happened before the game and it stunned the Rangers' fans in the thirty thousand crowd ...

It also had a bad psychological effect on the players. The players were warming up. They were shooting in at goal when Colin Stein blasted in a shot which Peter McCloy tried to stop. The giant goalkeeper's hand was bent back and then down he went in agony. There were only minutes to go until kick off time as Jock Wallace and Tommy Craig raced to see McCloy. Almost immediately they knew that the wrist was probably broken and that McCloy could not play. Hurriedly Stewart Kennedy stripped off his track suit and took over – his first major competitive ap-pearance since his traumatic experience against England at Wembley. The freak accident made it hard for Rangers to settle. They were shaky in their defensive strategy, unsure of themselves after the pre-match jinx which had robbed them of their first choice 'keeper.

And in twenty-eight minutes Rochetau and Revelli – the two men Wallace had pin-pointed combined to get the first goal. Rocheteau lured Alex Miller out of position before crossing for Revelli to hammer a shot into the net.

That goal hauled Rangers together, though. They tightened the defence, they began to move the ball neatly in midfield and on occasions they broke to worry Piazza and his fellow defenders.

Suddenly they were playing the way Wallace had wanted them to play.

The shock at the loss of McCloy had gone. Professionally they had decided to get on with the job and gradually they appeared to be wearing down the Frenchmen. St Etienne battered away at the Rangers' defence but there were few moments to trouble the Scots.

On the other hand after Cutty Young and Martin Henderson replaced Derek Parlane and Tommy McLean the Ibrox men twice threatened St Etienne's Yugoslav goalkeeper Ivan Curkovic. Alex MacDonald had a brilliant header saved by the Slav and then six minutes from the end Colin Jackson upfield for a cor-ner kick headed the ball into the net. But Colin Stein had pushed a defender and a freekick was given against Rangers. Still, it had been close and with the score still 1–0 hopes soared for the second leg at Ibrox.

Then came the second blow. A tragedy for Alex MacDonald who had worked tirelessly in midfield. There was a minute to go when he tried to push a short pass back to Sandy Jardine standing behind him. The ball did not make it as Dominique Bathenay brushed past MacDonald, reached the ball before Jardine and then sent it past Stewart Kennedy and into the net. MacDonald fell to the turf in despair – because that goal changed the whole complexion of the tie. Now Rangers needed three goals to win at Ibrox. A tall order against such experienced opposition.

A glum Wallace admitted: 'We had the game in our grasp. We lost our goalkeeper before a ball was kicked in anger. We had a goal disallowed and then they score in the last seconds of the game. It was cruel because we were so close to a great result!'

Wallace, typically, would not blame anyone. But MacDonald accepted the blame himself. He felt that he had caused the defeat and only his League Cup winning goal three days later eased his hurt. (He describes that goal and what it meant in another chapter.)

Anyhow, Rangers were up against it now and they knew it. That fatal lapse made an enormous difference in European terms – but between the two games Rangers won the League Cup and then drew with Celtic at Parkhead. These results boosted their confidence again and at their pre-match HQ at Largs Wallace asked the fans: 'Get behind us – because if you do then you can help us win the game. They helped us win the Cup Winners Cup with the support they gave us. They are the best in Europe and this game could be swung by them. If we can score early then we could have the French on the run.'

Looking for the goals he needed Wallace decided to give a key role to Derek Johnstone. The multi-talented youngster – he defends, plays in midfield, and strikes with equal authority – was to be pushed forward. Rangers wanted to use his heading power inside the penalty box. Wallace felt that with Tommy McLean there to pinpoint crosses onto Johnstone's head Rangers could win. In a way the tactics are old-fashioned – but against most Continental teams they remain effective.

St Etienne arrived brimming with confidence. It was a stark contrast to how they might have been if only Rangers had not conceded that second goal – and Manager Herbin admitted as much. He said: 'The second goal in our stadium was the decisive one. Until then we were in great danger. Now it should be enough to take us into the quarter finals.'

Forty-five thousand fans turned out on Guy Fawkes night expecting football fireworks. Unhappily they did not arrive . . . at least, not from Rangers. They hurled themselves forward into attack after attack. They did break through once in the first half when Curkovic dived to save a Derek Parlane header . . . but the

The coup-de-grâce is applied at Ibrox in the European Cup
second leg match. St Etienne forward Herve Revelli goes through
to score with the Ibrox defence wide open. Stewart Kennedy and
Sandy Jardine are the two helpless Rangers.

St Etienne defence built around the solid Piazza gave nothing away. They coped with Derek Johnstone in the air and they found gaps in the Rangers' defence as the Scots went hell-for-leather after goals.

It was the kind of game where Rangers were bound to leave openings, the kind of game where it was all or nothing at all. They had to get goals – but they failed. Instead they left themselves open for counter punches from the French. Rocheteau broke free down the wing in sixty-three minutes, went on almost unchallenged and then shot past Stewart Kennedy – still in goal while McCloy was injured – for the opener. By then the fans knew that their dreams of Europe glory had been killed. When Rocheteau set off down the wing again and made a chance for Herve Revelli – the brother of the first leg scorer – to get the second it was over. Rangers had been beaten in front of their own fans. Thousands of them had left for home when Alex Mac-Donald eventually scored a goal in the closing minute. It was scant consolation for the Scots who had wanted to do well in Europe. Out they went on a 4–1 aggregate and St Etienne marched on to meet Dynamo Kiev in the quarter finals.

The difficult draw – and, make no mistake, St Etienne were difficult opponents – came just a little too soon for Rangers. It came when they had off form players. Too many of them were out of touch at the same time.

Another easy draw, perhaps just that stage above Bohemians would have been ideal. However it was not to be their year in Europe and Jock Wallace found it hard to mask his disappoinment. It was even more painful than usual because of those cruel tricks of fate which hit Rangers in the first leg game in France. And also because so many of the players had felt they would be able to beat the Frenchmen – even with the two goal lead they brought with them to Ibrox.

Several of them told me: 'They are not as good as Sporting Lisbon or Torino or Bayern. They are well organized, clever – but they can be beaten and we can do it.'

Sadly, though, Rangers did not hit form and that night at Ibrox was one of the low points in their season.

The players knew that better than anyone . . .

THE BACKROOM BOYS-
TOMMY CRAIG AND
JOE MASON

Last season Rangers hauled three players from the obscurity of their reserve team to become regulars in the League side.

Alex Miller took his chance when Sandy Jardine was injured and established himself as a dogged and determined full back . . .

Johnny Hamilton, that one-time discard from Hibs, became a guiding figure in the midfield which was so productive for Rangers in the latter part of the season . . .

And, of course, up front Martin Henderson did the same as Miller – took his chance when injury forced Derek Parlane out of the team.

It isn't always the case that reserve teams can throw up players in this way. At Ibrox it has become a priority with Manager Jock Wallace and his backroom boys that players MUST be available to replace injured first team men. And off the elegant marble hallway, down the long corridor past the treatment room and the dressing room is the trainer's room where so many of the decisions which shape the team are taken.

It was there I talked with reserve team coach Joe Mason and physiotherapist Tom Craig – the men Wallace describes as 'the best backroom team in the business'. They are the men whose advice he listens to – then either accepts or rejects it.

The final decision is his alone and depending on circumstances it goes the way he has been advised – or the way his own hunches tell him. But always there is discussion with the downstairs team – the 'kitchen cabinet' of Ibrox if you like.

'And,' stresses Craig, 'there are no holds barred. There is no point in simply saying what the gaffer wants to hear and he has told us this. He wants our opinions about players' fitness or attitudes or anything else which may carry him into the first team to do a specific job. There is a lot of hard, hard talking. We don't always agree because in this game everyone has their own opinions. The thing is we talk it all out . . .'

Added Mason: 'I don't see the first team so very often because, naturally, I'm with the reserves almost all the time they are play-

Alex O'Hara, one of the youngsters being guided back to peak form by Tommy Craig and Joe Mason, the Ibrox backroom boys.

ing. Sometimes, though, I see them and because I've been away for a while I can spot something that is maybe going just a wee bit wrong. It's the same when the gaffer comes to see the reserves. He can get things home to me – and he does. The only thing is we usually lose when he and Tom are both able to come and see us and the first team isn't playing. They're jinxing us!'

That was a Mason joke because no one has been doing very much 'jinxing' on a Rangers' reserve team which has been so successful over the past few seasons. And successful in different ways. Successful in winning trophies – and successful in bringing players through into the first team.

'Obviously the main job is to prepare players for the first team,' admits Mason. 'At the same time you can never forget that it's Rangers who are playing and there is no way you want to accept a defeat. You have to keep going for victory whether it's in reserves or first team.

'Of course, the whole thing at Ibrox is that the reserve team is important in all planning. There is no way that players are ignored because they aren't in the first team pool. Everyone watches their progress in the second team, everyone at the club wants to know how the reserves are doing. I get lads like Alex Miller coming into training and they're able to speak to me about how far in front we are in the reserve championship race. They may have left the reserves and broken through to the first team – but they don't forget the lads. Or the team itself.'

The emphasis on the reserve team power has come since Jock Wallace's appointment as coach under the managership of Willie Waddell. Tom Craig joined the club as the new regime took over.

He recalls: 'We knew we had a lot of work on our hands but right away I remember that the youth team went abroad to play in a tournament run by Ajax in Holland. That was the start of the fresh system . . . one which prepares young players to face up to the realities of European football as early as possible. Derek Johnstone was there and Derek Parlane and look how they have come on since then.

'Basically, I think the boss decided to rear his own players. And the way the system works here anyone who comes through it and reaches the first team has proved himself. Naturally I'm more involved on the physical side. We started weight training in a big way – and we still do it. But it built these lads into men. They had circuits set out where they were asked to lift something like five thousand pounds. There was no way any of them were excused that. The boss wanted them strong. Take Peter McCloy – he was always big but he wasn't carrying enough weight.

'He could be knocked about by forwards when he came out for a ball. We succeeded in putting weight on him and there is no one who'll knock him about now.'

Johnstone, though, is probably the finest product of the system so far. He was there when it all began and has blossomed into a player Jock Wallace describes as 'the best in Britain'.

Recalls Craig: 'Derek broke through early as a striker because he had this amazing ability in the air. It was 'Roy of the Rovers' stuff, if you remember. Sixteen years old and he scored the goal against Celtic which won Rangers the League Cup. That took some doing But he had a bad spell after that. He went out of the team and he even dropped in form so badly that he went out of the reserve team as well. It was all too much for him. No one at that age can play sixty first team games for Rangers. You must remember the demands placed on players at Ibrox. They are expected to win every week. Defeat is a disaster for the fans and this puts pressure on players. Some withstand it better than others but you have to watch carefully to see which lads will stand up best. When you have young players then they have to be coaxed through it – or maybe bullied through it. The Boss finds all that out in these talks we have, how best to handle the different players. He is successful with them too. Anyhow, as I was saying big Derek went off and we had to be patient and nurse him through that spell. Then back he came and it's hard to believe that he did have a bad time. It was a natural thing to happen to a young player.'

Alex O'Hara, another teenage wonder boy who stepped into the first team and immediately began grabbing goals and head-lines, has had the same kind of problem. Mason, in charge of the reserves, draws a parallel between the two players He points out: 'Alex was exactly the same as big Derek. He burst into the team, he scored goals as a striker and he was brilliant in the air. Then out he went and he had an injury or two and he lost a bit of form. Again he wasn't always in the second team. But we have had to work away with him because we know he has the ability to come back. He doesn't lose that. These are temporary phases in the development of a player. We have had Alex in midfield. at centre half and he has regained the confidence he lost for a spell. Really it helps to move them around sometimes. The same thing happened with Derek, too. I'm not saying it's the answer to every player. But we like to try lads out in different positions because it adds to their vision of the game. Ian McDougall has played in midfield, at full back and at sweeper. Others have had the same kind of preparation but young Chris Robertson is just an out and out striker. There is no other place for that laddie. He has to be up front looking for goals – and he gets them.

'The tremendous thing about all of them, though, is that they are always ready to come back and work extra hard. They'll be there in the afternoons brushing up on things, trying to improve all the time. It makes our job so much easier with that attitude.'

Some players have natural strengths in their game and these are what the Rangers' staff work on. Tom Craig remembers: 'With Derek Johnstone we worked and worked and worked on his heading – not because he had a weakness there – but the opposite.

'You see Mr Waddell made the point pretty forcibly once and I'll always remember it. He didn't want us working on a weakness all the time – he wanted us to work on Derek's strengths. He had this natural ability in the air and so we made that even better and he is almost unbeatable now. We worked on the strong points to make them even stronger. It works.'

It works, also, producing mainly your own players. Of last year's regulars the home-bred men were Miller, and Henderson mentioned earlier, plus Derek Parlane, Sandy Jardine. John Greig. Colin Jackson, Derek Johnstone. Others are ready to break through. Says Mason: 'I came here as a player from another club and I know how hard it is to settle in. And we have had one or two others recently. There was Kenny Watson from Montrose. Now he took time in the reserves to find his feet. It's not surprising. This is a big, big club and when you come from somewhere else you feel that whenever you come through the front door. It's happened that way all down through the years. The lads who have been bought have found it difficult.'

'Anyhow when they come as youngsters they take to the disci-

(a) Derek Johnstone was one of the first players to come through the new regime at Ibrox. But he lost his way for a spell, too, just like O'Hara. Here though he knows exactly where he is going as he beats John Murphy (left) and Rikki Fleming of Ayr United.

(b) Alex Miller is one of the players who graduated from the reserves but still likes to keep in touch with their progress. Here he comes through with the ball in an 'Old Firm' game. The player he is leaving behind is Kenny Dalglish the Celtic skipper.

plining more easily,' broke in Craig. 'They are told that they are expected to wear a collar and tie and all these small things which are important. Also, they learn from going abroad. These young players are off to some tournament or other every season. Holland, France, Italy, Portugal – they go and they learn about playing there. The boss is a great believer in all that. They don't just learn about football either. They learn about being good ambassadors for the club and for Scotland, too.

'Last close-season when we were short of players for the round-the-world trip because of international calls on the players, two of the youngsters went along. Martin Henderson and Alastair Dawson were the two and they knew the ropes from the start. They didn't have to have anything explained to them because they had both been away with the reserves before.'

'Well,' explained Mason, 'we try to follow the same routine

abroad as the big team does. We like to have a pretty strict code of behaviour and I follow what the gaffer does with the top team. If it works there then it has to work with us. The lads then grow up with the club knowing what is expected from them on and off the field.'

I asked how promotion to the first team came about. Replied Mason: 'The great thing is that a player who is playing well in the reserves will get his chance. I mean, like last season when Derek Parlane broke his collar bone I didn't have any hesitation about saying that Martin Henderson was ready to go in. The Boss realized that anyhow because he had had him on the bench quite a few times. But, what I'm getting at is that there isn't simply a player pool being shuffled around so that youngsters don't get their chance. That happens in many teams and it can be discouraging to players in the second teams. It doesn't happen at Ibrox. They all get a chance. It's good that it does happen.'

Added Craig: 'This is really Joe's pigeon though maybe the Boss will ask me how the player has been doing on the circuits or at some other aspect of training. But the basic point that Joe hammered in there is the right one. Players do get their chance. No one can leave here and say they didn't get the opportunity. If they do go away from the club then it's probably because they were not good enough.

'It isn't easy for players here. It isn't meant to be easy. They have to reach very high standards. If they don't then they move on – sometimes to other clubs.'

Quickly Joe Mason came in to underline this – 'Yes and when they do we like to think that they will be assets to that club because of what we have tried to teach them here. We work hard with them. Not everyone can stay. But when they go they have a lot of good things taught to them. They leave as better players and, I believe, better men, too.'

One of the major surprises last year was the emergence of Johnny Hamilton as a regular in the Premier League side. Hamilton had been signed on a free transfer from Hibs. His signing had been a gamble and when he languished in the reserves it looked as if the gamble had failed for Jock Wallace. Then came the breakthrough. I asked Mason if he had been as surprised as most of the supporters. 'Nothing in this game surprises me,' he smiled. 'Hammy was a good player. He had skill, lots of skill, and in the reserves he was a key man for us. He was great with the younger players around him. But when you have natural skills, when you are a good footballer then nothing should stop you getting into the first team. He had these skills and I think he proved it. I wasn't surprised – and I was pleased for him.'

94

The job is, of course, winning games – but it is also, as I mentioned earlier, keeping a conveyor belt of talent available for the first team. With that in mind I asked both the backroom boys their tips for stardom – the reserves they looked to for a breakthrough into the first team squad. They came up with the same two names . . .

Said Mason: 'Ally Dawson is one and the other is Chris Robertson – because he has a great goal touch. They are only eighteen but if the Boss asked me tomorrow for players for the first team I'd recommend them.'

And Craig echoed: 'I'd take the same two as Joe from what I've seen of them. And Ally Dawson proved himself on the world tour, after all. He played a few games there and he was in the first team once or twice at the start of the season until he was injured. He has shown it already.'

Finally, Joe Mason had a word about one more of his charges – Kenny Watson the midfield man bought from Montrose last season. 'He is coming right after taking six months or so to adapt to the whole new environment,' he told me. 'We moved him around a bit too, playing him as a 'sweeper' in the youth tournament in Viareggio for example. But he is a midfield player and he is improving all the time. A settling-in period was essential to him. Now he is coming through. Watch out for him along with the others.'

These are this year's tips – next year there could be more. The search for new talent is endless and unrelenting. Rangers work on their young players with a small backroom staff. It's the way Jock Wallace wants it. He reckons that too many coaches would be a bit like too many cooks . . .

And he adds his own tribute: 'I can work with Tom and Joe because now after being together for a while we are on the same wavelength. They know what I am looking for. They know what kind of players I want for the first team and they know what the club requires, too. That is what it is all about. If the players keep coming through the way the Johnstones and Parlanes and Hendersons came through then we will be happy.'

Not just happy, either, but probably successful as well. The Rangers successes seem to date from the time they began to concentrate on home-grown talent. It's not that they will refuse to buy players – they bought Bobby McKean and Tom Forsyth and Peter McCloy and Tommy McLean and Alex MacDonald – but basically the pattern has changed. They would rather breed their own stars. The emphasis is on players coming through from the 'S' form signings and the trial games that are held at Ibrox for these schoolboys, through to the Continental youth tournaments and then into the reserves. The rest is up to them but if they qualify from this soccer finishing school at Ibrox then Wallace and the two man team in that trainer's room will be talking about first team promotions regularly!

Backroom boy Tommy Craig is in trouble in this sequence of pictures and the referee he tangled with is World Cup whistler Bobby Davidson.

Tommy Craig is on the park to treat an injured Derek Johnstone – but the referee wants him off.

As Craig continues treatment the referee reaches for his notebook.

The card comes out now as Craig still tries to revive Johnstone with Rangers players Colin Jackson (left) and Derek Parlane watching.

Finally Craig carries Johnstone from the field for further treatment and the incident is closed. . . .

THE FIRST PREMIER LEAGUE CHAMPIONS
by John Greig

Last season was the first of a new look Scottish League set-up, a change in the composition of the League which brought a Top Ten into being. This was the Premier League – a league we were determined to win from the start of the year. And one we eventually did win just before the season's end. It meant a great deal to us, not simply another championship (though that was fine), but the chance to be the very FIRST champions in the Premier League.

Believe me, too, it was difficult to win that title. The set-up was the most competitive it had ever been in Scotland. There we were, the ten best clubs based on the placings of the previous season, and we had to meet each other four times during the season before new champions were crowned. That meant four games against Celtic, four games against Hibs, four more against Hearts and Aberdeen and Dundee and Dundee United and so on.

We realized early on that picking up easy points was just not on. This was the League which shut up all those who have scoffed at the Scottish First Division being less competitive than other leagues. There is no way anyone can call this an easy League. I admit it – in the old set-up there used to be games where you would go away from home expecting to win both points. It didn't always happen that way but most of the time it did and these games were not exciting enough to keep the fans happy. Last season that was all changed.

This was a League which pleased the fans and the players at the same time.

We found ourselves facing more competitive games and that is something which should make all of us better players . . .

The fans saw the standard of football rise and they also saw entertaining matches. There were far fewer meaningless games

Rangers' skipper John Greig holds the Championship trophy aloft after his team have been crowned as the first Premier League Champions.

than before. Just take a look at the climax of the season and you can see that. Everything, apart from St Johnstone's drop to the First Division, was kept until the last week of the season. That was when the title was won, the European placings were decided and the other team for relegation was determined.

Yet, in all this talk about the success of the new League and of our own success in winning it, I'm still convinced that it was a defeat which made us champions. A defeat which came in the European Cup, incidentally, and not in the League.

That was when we lost to St Etienne, the champions of France, who went on to lose so unluckily by 1–0 to Bayern Munich of West Germany in the European Cup Final at Hampden. We played the Frenchmen in the second round of the tournament and we lost to them. We were knocked out of Europe and we were in the middle of a bad spell in the League. All that held us together was a victory in the League Cup Final over Celtic. Our championship hopes seemed to be fading . . . Europe was a memory . . . and it was then the Boss (Jock Wallace) knew he had to change the team around. I think, too, most of the lads realized that we had to buckle down if we were going to hold onto the League Championship trophy!

We were struggling before that European result made us all have a re-think. Results had gone badly and I had a nagging fear then that Hibs were going to be champions. Strangely, enough, Celtic were never the biggest worry for me.

Hibs were the team I thought might break through. They had been on the verge for a season or two. They had good players, just as talented as the players anywhere else in Scotland and there was a special look about them early on in the season that had me worried.

I was wrong, of course. Celtic did emerge as the biggest threat and Motherwell won themselves the honour of team of the year in my book. They sneaked into the Top Ten by the skin of their teeth at the end of the season before. They had shown some flashes, some brief glimpses of good play but nothing sustained. I couldn't see them challenging but how they surprised and impressed me and probably everyone else in football too.

They stayed in the League race for a long, long time and they reached the semi-final of the Scottish Cup where they gave us a bit of a fright. Most of the credit for that has to go to the manager, Willie McLean, who is the older brother of our Tommy at

Rangers had to face 'Old Firm' rivals Celtic four times last season. In this match off-field mates, Sandy Jardine (Rangers) and Kenny Dalglish (Celtic), tangle.

Ibrox. He had the backing of his board and out he went to spend money on players. He bought Colin McAdam from Dumbarton, Willie McVie from Clyde, Peter Marinello from Portsmouth and picked up Vic Davidson from Celtic on a free transfer. Then towards the end of the season he bought again when he made another signing from Celtic – ex-Scotland goalkeeper Alastair Hunter. These were gambles – any provincial club spending that way is gambling. Yet they paid off for Willie McLean and his club I'm glad to say. The crowds came back to see them. We played to one very big crowd at Fir Park in the second half of the season – possibly the biggest I've ever played in front of there. Now that meant something to me. It spelled out that the fans wanted to see the kind of football that we were providing and the kind of ambition that Motherwell possessed. They wanted to go somewhere, do something, win something.

In the end they were unfortunate. They missed out on the prizes and we had to produce something extra to stop them in that Scottish Cup semi-final at Hampden. However, the major point is that they were the team of the year for me because of the ambition and improvement they showed. This is what the Premier League helped to bring about.

Anyhow, to get back to ourselves. I do believe that the St Etienne game set us on the road to the title. It was after changes were made that the team settled to hit our best form. We began a run before Christmas and stayed unbeaten until the end of the season. It was a tremendous performance and yet even with us being able to do that we could not catch up on Celtic. They were ahead and they were determined to stay there. Obviously they wanted to be the first Premier League champions just as we did. And so week after week, game after game, we pushed our unbeaten run longer and longer and saw Celtic remain on top. It was hard to take but we knew that we had to hang on and wait for a break. Then the breaks began to come all at once as we maintained our pressure. While we kept on getting points, vital points, Celtic started to lose them. Then when the end came it came suddenly. One week we overhauled them at the top to nose in front by a single point and the following week we were champions.

The game which brought us the title was unexpected. We were at Tannadice playing Dundee United while Celtic were at home to Ayr United. The teams we faced were both heavily involved in the relegation struggle and we knew that points would be

And here in another match, Greig himself moves in to clear from Celtic veteran attacker Bobby Lennox.

Greig thought Motherwell were the 'shock' team of the season.
Here you see two of their buys in action against Rangers. Colin
McAdam moves in to tackle Alex MacDonald while Willie McVie
is in the background with Martin Henderson.

John Greig, named Player of the Year by the Scottish Football
Writers' Association, thought ex-Rangers midfield man Bobby
Watson, who was with Motherwell, might have been nominated.
Here Watson, who announced his retirement at the end of the
season, gets ready to challenge Alex MacDonald.

difficult to get. We expected to struggle – and we did have it hard even though Derek Johnstone sent us into the lead after only twenty-five seconds' play. Celtic, though, had it tougher. They lost to Ayr United and the title came to us.

It happened all wrong, of course. The championship was supposed to be decided two days later when we were set to meet Celtic at Celtic Park. Everyone was looking for that to be the big showdown. Football, however, is a funny game. So many things are expected and so many times it all goes wrong. For ourselves, the players, it didn't matter. We were champions and it didn't matter where we won the crown. Doing it at Tannadice was unexpected – but it brought just as much pleasure to us.

Of course, we had the usual roars from the crowd telling us that Celtic were in trouble. It's amazing nowadays. So many thousands of people seem to have transistor radios at the games and if anything big is happening the news soon reaches us. We had an idea it was going right for us but it wasn't until we were in the dressing room that we knew for certain. Then out we went for that lap of honour the fans had waited to see.

That title realized all the dreams I had had for the season and then the Cup came as an extra bonus to make a 'treble'. It seemed unbelievable. Let's face it there had been doubts cast about my fitness when the season opened. People remembered how I had been plagued by injury the year before and wondered if I would break down again. Luckily it all went the other way. I played in every Rangers game and even managed to fit in another one with Scotland – all of that on top of the close season tour. It was that trip which set me up, of course. I had the chance there to play myself in and then for the rest of the summer I stayed in training and that was it.

To play in all the games, though, was an extra prize. I did not expect that. Nor did I expect two more goodies which came my way – being chosen again for Scotland and being named Player of the Year by the Scottish Football Writers' Association.

Taking them one at a time – getting the 'cap' was something very special. I'd played so many times for Scotland and been a regular for many years when suddenly in 1971 I went out of the team and just never got the chance to get back in. I guess that's the way it happens in international teams. One year you're a regular – the next you're out in the cold. Well, that was it with me when last season I received the call back into the team for one game. It came because of call-offs, the problem which always seems to trouble Scotland sides. This time, though, it helped me. It was the day we had won the League Cup and I was at home when I was phoned by a newspaperman who told me the news that Martin Buchan of Manchester United had withdrawn because of injury and that the Scotland team manager Willie Ormond had decided to pull me into the squad.

So there I was at the age of thirty-three making an international comeback. It wasn't in any old game either. It was against Denmark in a European Championship match. I was made captain and we won the game. Eventually, of course, Spain qualified from the section. But we did what we had to do that night at Hampden and I was delighted. It gave me the chance, the personal opportunity, if you like, to prove to people that I could still handle myself at the very top level. I enjoyed being with the lads, as well. There wasn't anyone left from my days in the team but it was good to meet up with old mates like Archie Gemmill and meet the new lads like wee Archie's Derby pal Bruce Rioch. I was impressed with a lot of the players and I do think Scotland has a good chance of qualifying for the World Cup Finals again with the current squad.

As for yours truly winning the Player of the Year award – well, I was honestly surprised. I had won it before, ten years earlier to be exact, and I thought some of the other players would get it this time around. When I was told that I had won I sat and thought about it. If I had been given it simply as the captain of the team which won the treble, as one man being used to honour a team performance, then I would have felt guilty. But I realized that it had been an exceptional season for me. Playing in all the games . . . winning that 'cap' again . . . all of it rolled together and so I decided to savour the joy of winning the award once more.

It was a good feeling, too. Maybe it will be an inspiration to some of the other older players who are still in the game. Sometimes I think that players are written off far too early in this country – and I'm not saying that because I'm on the wrong side of thirty myself. I've felt it for a while. On the Continent they don't see 30 as a disaster age for players and it should be the same here.

Of course, the other players at Ibrox helped me get it. I know that. Without them, all of them, Rangers wouldn't have won the three major honours and my own season would be so much less memorable than it turned out to be.

Yet, when I was thinking about winning the award, I drew up a list of players I would have been happy to see winning it. (I know that I'm not allowed to vote, that it's a Football Writers' award, but we all have our little daydreams, don't we?).

So here we go, with five players I would have been ready to

vote for if I was a writer and I've given my reasons why I admire the players so much, too.

For a kick-off I'm staying with the over-thirty club and naming Bobby Graham of Motherwell. He was just a little bit forgotten by so many people last season because Willie Pettigrew scored all the goals and grabbed all the headlines. Graham, though, the ex-Liverpool and Coventry City player, was the man supplying most of the ammunition. He was doing it with style and with skill. Bobby picked up a lot of experience down south and then came to Motherwell when Ian St John his old Anfield team-mate was manager. Now he uses all his experience and I'm sure Willie Pettigrew would agree with me when I say Bobby was outstanding last year. His influence at Motherwell was very special . . .

Then to show I'm not biased, and only looking after old friends, I would nominate a new boy – Malcolm Robertson of Ayr United. He had been with Raith Rovers for quite a few

Here Greig and goalkeeper Peter McCloy foil another of Greig's 'nominees' – Motherwell veteran Bobby Graham who looks on as the Ibrox pair mop up this attack.

years and no one from a top club had signed him. Then Alex Stuart bought him after he had been appointed Ayr United manager. Alex, the ex-Montrose boss had seen a lot of Robertson in his Second Division days. He liked him, took the chance and signed him. Robertson looked so good that when John Doyle was sold to Celtic the Ayr fans scarcely realized what had happened. He has skill and he moves well all the time, refusing to be tied down by a defender. He pops up on either wing and causes trouble on both sides. When we played them towards the end of the season we used Alex Miller as a marker and he gave Alex a difficult time of it. I was very impressed with him. This coming year I'd look for him becoming even better because he is going to move house to Ayr and cutting out travelling will help him.

Then I would have gone to the Scotland squad and taken out one of the most dedicated professionals I've met – Celtic right back Danny McGrain. In fact, Danny was runner-up to me in the actual voting among the writers. He had a tremendous season for Celtic and when I was with that Scotland squad in training at Seamill before the international I was very impressed with him. He is a thorough professional and he is a player I've always admired.

After Danny I'm back at the 'old fellas' again . . . and back to Motherwell, too. Bobby Watson is a player I would have liked to see being honoured in some way because he has given so much to the game. He was at Ibrox with me and then moved to Fir Park where he has been a great servant. Now he has decided to retire. He's younger than me, too!! Bobby is only thirty but he has decided to leave football and concentrate on his business. I know that most of the players in the game will agree with me that he will be missed. It won't seem the same going to play against Motherwell without Bobby lining up against you.

Finally, I'm at Ayr United for the second nomination from their team too. Again, I'm praising Manager Alex Stuart's shrewd buying sense. He went to Perth and bought Gordon Cramond from St Johnstone. Again this was a player he knew because he had sold Cramond from Montrose to St Johnstone. This little fellow reminds me so much of Archie Gemmill, it's not true. He is small and he has the same fire that Archie has – and the skill to go with it. I'll never forget a game last year when we went to Perth and won 5–1. It was one of our best displays of the season and we really turned it on.

A familiar sight as Rangers went towards their first Premier League title – celebration over Celtic. Sandy Jardine salutes in triumph as Rangers remain unbeaten against their old rivals. Celtic did not win one of the 'Old Firm' games during the season.

Hibs' skipper Pat Stanton shields the ball from young Rangers
striker Martin Henderson – Stanton's team was the one Greig
feared most in the title race.

Yet it isn't our own performance that comes back to me most forcibly about that afternoon at Muirton – it's Gordon Cramond's. He had just recovered from 'flu I remember and had more or less risen from his sick bed to play against us. And how he played! He refused to give in. He chased us and he harried us and he kept at his own players trying to lift them as well. He fought hard that day and like I say, I just always think of wee Archie whenever I see him – and I have a very high opinion of Archie Gemmill's talent so that is a big compliment to another player who is too often overlooked. Maybe at Ayr he will get a little bit more recognition than he managed to get at Perth. I hope so because he deserves it.

These were some of the players who impressed me in the Premier League games last year. Motherwell, were the team who impressed me most, and Hibs were the disappointment. Somehow or other I keep looking for them to break through. They were the team I feared most last year when the season started and yet they slumped badly to third place in the League and lost to Motherwell in the quarter finals of the Scottish Cup. Something went wrong, which can happen to any team, and so they didn't run us nearly as close as I expected. Hibs, I suppose, always had a kind of Indian sign on Rangers. They were the team who would be able to beat us even when we were going strongly. Last year, of course, they didn't find it so easy. I think it was when we beat them soon after the New Year, in a match at Ibrox, that I felt we were heading for the title.

We had beaten Celtic for the second time at Ibrox and our confidence was mounting. When we clinched the Hibs game, too, I couldn't see anyone stopping us. Then we also had a useful victory at Fir Park and the wins against the three other leading teams consolidated our belief in ourselves.

That belief grew stronger and stronger as the season went on and the Boss worked on it. He even took us up to Dunkeld for a week-end golf break after a game at Perth. That helped keep the dressing-room atmosphere just right. The secret at Ibrox is in that dressing room. The spirit is great and we are well aware of how important that is to the club. Any success we have comes from the feeling that is generated amongst us all, day after day.

I remember when Iain Munro joined us from Hibs. He came into training for the first time, heard the patter from the lads, watched us get on with the training and marvelled at it all. He told me later that he'd never known a better dressing-room atmosphere. I agree with the Boss 100 per cent about this. He believes a strong team has to come from a happy dressing room and so do I. This is the happiest dressing room I've ever been in so maybe there are going to be some more successes on the way for us. I'd like to think so. It would be nice to add another medal or two before I have to retire. Not that I'm thinking about it yet. I suppose I'll know when the time comes. Now, though, after a long season I feel as fit as I have ever felt. During the season, too, I can't say I found myself feeling any strain.

I'd admit to being a little bit worried at one stage of the League race. We were on that long unbeaten run but didn't seem able to overtake Celtic. Just then I had some worrying moments but always at the back of my mind was the thought that we had still to play Celtic once more in the League and that we would win that game if it was going to mean the title. As it happened, of course, the final clash with Celtic was meaningless. We had already won the title and the match ended in a 0–0 draw. I think the thing most fans remember from that match was Derek Johnstone's display at centre-half.

These are some of the memories I will have, too, from the first year of the Premier League. It was an important year for all of us in Scottish football because it was a year of change. The changes that were made, though, brought success – or at least I felt that they did. The game was better. Obviously there is sadness in seeing clubs go down after one season and especially a club with the tradition of Dundee. I've played on Dens Park every year since I joined the Rangers first team and now I won't be there any longer because Dundee dropped to the First Division. That's sad but some clubs had to go down and basically the whole of the Premier League has benefited from the increased competition.

I was just happy that I was still there to take part in it and finally to get another championship medal. It is one I'll prize above all the others because it came from such a memorable season . . .

HAMPDEN BELONGED TO RANGERS

Skipper John Greig is hoisted
on his team-mates'
shoulders as he kisses the
Scottish Cup – last trophy
in the Rangers grand slam.
Bobby McKean, Alex Miller and
Martin Henderson are the players
holding Greig. Others in the
picture are left to right – Alex
MacDonald, Johnny Hamilton
and Sandy Jardine.

The game has been going just forty-two seconds and Rangers are in front in the 1976 Scottish Cup Final. Derek Johnstone (11) the goal-scorer, races to salute the fans while Colin Jackson (5) chases after him. The Hearts players are Jim Jefferies (4), Sandy Burrell (3) and Roy Kay on the ground.

The Scottish Football Association decided against making the Scottish Cup Final of 1976 an all-ticket occasion. Instead they left parts of the terracing at Hampden open to those fans who decided to turn up on the day . . .

The result was a massive attendance of 85 000 – two hundred and fifty higher than the new crowd limit set by the police on Glasgow's biggest ground. And that day, May 1, Hampden belonged to Rangers and their fans.

The Ibrox men clinched the treble with a 3–1 win over Hearts which began when the remarkable Derek Johnstone scored after only forty-two seconds' play.

And afterwards Rangers' vice-chairman Willie Waddell declared happily: 'Our fans were magnificent today. They stood and they cheered the team on to victory and they made the Final an occasion.

'We asked them to do this. We made a plea in the club's newspaper to the supporters to show the world that our Cup Final was a very special affair. They did us proud.'

Hampden was a sea of royal blue as Rangers swept to victory and yet a month before the 'treble' had looked an impossible dream for Jock Wallace and his men. That, though, is getting ahead of ourselves. The Scottish Cup campaign had kicked off back at the end of January and Rangers were handed a home draw against First Division East Fife. It was the kind of tie they wanted to start with, an easy looking one at home and that's the way it turned out in front of 24 000 supporters. Little East Fife did have a chance in the early minutes – then Rangers took over,

In thirteen minutes Tommy McLean slipped a free kick to Alex MacDonald who scored, and thirteen minutes later young Martin Henderson scored a second. The game was finished then but Johnny Hamilton made it worthwhile for the fans who waited until the end by scoring the third in eighty-three minutes. That was Rangers through and within ten minutes they knew the draw for the next round – and they had a hard one.

Aberdeen were their opponents, a Pittodrie team who had suddenly found themselves after Ally McLeod had been appointed as manager. McLeod, the voluble, long-time manager of Ayr United had left the part-time Somerset Park club to take over the ambitious Aberdeen. He had the players fighting for him and they were convinced that they would be able to hold Rangers and force a replay on their own ground.

McLeod made confident noises before the tie. 'We have played Rangers already,' he declared, 'and we don't see anything to fear from them. OK they are having a good run but so are we! That levels all that out and I feel my players are ready to break through in this competition. We want this game and we can get to the next round!'

It was typical fighting talk from McLeod while Jock Wallace withdrew quietly and left him holding the stage. Wallace, too, knew it would be one of the best ties in the Cup and he looked for the fans turning out to support the team. Again the Ibrox legions did not let him down. Fifty-three thousand were at Ibrox and they saw one of Rangers' most thoroughly professional demolition jobs of the season. They won 4–1 and before the end the Aberdeen team had been convincingly destroyed.

Rangers took over the game. While Aberdeen made it plain that they were going to rely on defence – and tough defence at that – Rangers moved forward into wave after wave of attacks. Two Aberdeen players, Joe Smith and Davie Robb, were booked for fouls before Derek Johnstone, almost inevitably, gave Rangers the lead four minutes before half-time.

It was a typical Rangers goal. A long kick out from Peter McCloy was touched on by Bobby McKean and Johnstone moved onto the ball to score confidently. Then the killer goal arrived in forty-six minutes. Rangers kicked off in the second half and had the ball in the net before an Aberdeen player touched it. Martin Henderson pushed the ball to Tommy McLean out on the right. He gathered the ball, nursed it as he watched Alex MacDonald run into position and then chipped the ball forward as accurately as only he can. It practically landed on MacDonald's head and he glided it out of Andy Geogheghan's reach and into the net.

In seventy minutes Joe Smith did score for Aberdeen with a spectacular twenty yard shot and for a couple of minutes Rangers wavered. It was the only time in the game they looked uncomfortable and it didn't last too long. Martin Henderson scored in seventy-five minutes and Derek Parlane, who came on as a late substitute added the final touch with a shot for the fourth goal three minutes from the end.

And so Rangers marched on into the quarter finals and another clash with First Division opposition. This was a little bit different, though, from a home game against East Fife. It was a return match with Queen of the South, so shrewdly managed by former Celt Mike Jackson.

It was different from the East Fife game in a couple of ways. First of all it was to take place away from Ibrox at Queens' own ground in Dumfries, Palmerston Park. That just happened to be the place where Rangers had lost early in the season in a League Cup quarter-final tie. They had been beaten over ninety minutes in the second leg of the tie but gone on to win in extra time. Still, Queens were confident and Rangers' fans felt a little apprehension at the thought of the tight pitch and the ability Queens had shown there already.

The worries, though, proved groundless. This was Rangers in full flight and a sell-out crowd of 19 000 saw them in a glittering five-goal romp. Tommy McLean didn't score but he was one of the stars of this one. While other players struggled to control the ball in a swirling wind McLean was masterly. In thirty-seven minutes he set up the first goal for Bobby McKean and then did it again in seventy-one minutes. This time his perfect cross was headed by Martin Henderson, Queens' goalkeeper

This is number three for Rangers as Derek Johnstone shoots past the diving Jim Cruickshank and Jim Jefferies comes in too late with his tackle.

Here's where it all began — a game against lowly East Fife and
Derek Parlane has won this header with Martin Henderson looking
on. The man beaten in the jump is East Fife's Kojak, Tom Stevens.

Hearts' captain Jim Brown clashes here with Rangers' man of the
match Derek Johnstone and the ball spins clear.

The Cup run continued here and Derek Johnstone is scoring again. The victims this time are Aberdeen whose goalkeeper Andy Geogheghan is helpless as Johnstone scores.

Alan Ball clawed it clear and Derek Johnstone followed up to hammer the ball into the net. After that goal Queens collapsed and their giant-killing dreams became a rapidly fading memory. In seventy-five minutes Henderson scored, Derek Johnstone grabbed the fourth in seventy-eight minutes and then McKean rounded off the execution with the fifth goal in eighty-four minutes. It had been a slaughter with the four-goals-in-thirteen-minutes spell emphasizing the gulf between the two teams. It was hard for the fans to believe that on this ground their team had struggled so badly in the League Cup. But, then, this was a different Rangers, a fresh, confident Rangers who were chasing all the prizes!

Now they came to the BIG one. It was called the 'Final before the Final'. Just as in England when Derby County and Manchester United were drawn together, so in Scotland where Rangers were paired with the powerful Motherwell. The other semi-final between Hearts and Second Division Dumbarton was scarcely noticed. This was the glamour game, the one that the whole of Scotland had hoped to see at Hampden on Cup Final day. That was not to be, though. It was the semi-final pairing and one of the two teams had to go out . . .

And this was the game where Rangers came close to faltering on their way to the 'treble'! This was the game where they were given the fright of their lives by a Motherwell team who played with assurance and skill.

Forty-eight thousand people were at Hampden to watch the midweek match and they could scarcely believe it as they saw Rangers struggle against this Fir Park team. At half-time Rangers were two goals behind after Stewart McLaren and then the deadly Willie Pettigrew had scored goals for the outsiders. It seemed all over. The Pettigrew goal had come a minute before half-time – always such an important time to get a goal. There seemed no way that Rangers would come back.

Somehow, though, in the Hampden dressing room Jock Wallace worked one of his miracles. Somehow all the character that he had talked about so much shone through and somehow,

There was more glory in this one – a shot from the five-goal romp at Palmerston Park against Queen of the South. Alex MacDonald tries a shot as a Queens' defender steps in.

Rangers battled their way back into the game. And the man who won it for them was Derek Johnstone. First of all he was hauled down by goalkeeper Stewart Rennie after breaking clear of his 'shadow' defender Colin McAdam. Referee John Gordon awarded a penalty and Alex Miller scored. Then one of those long, long clearances from Peter McCloy panicked the opposing defence.

Again Johnstone was there, reading the flight of the ball correctly and heading the ball past Rennie as he came out of goal. And before the end Johnstone struck again with another header and Rangers had reached the Final.

The Motherwell players wept openly on their way back to the dressing room. They had been hit in a sensational second half by Rangers' secret weapon – the 'character' which Manager Jock Wallace insists his players have. Other teams would have given up. Rangers didn't. They fought on until they got the breaks they needed and Johnstone turned out the hero.

So there it was, the League coming close and the Cup within their grasp. No one could seriously see either Hearts or Dumbarton troubling Rangers. When the Second Division team held the Edinburgh side to a draw in the first game Rangers became even more odds-on certainties. Hearts went through in the replay but, by now, Rangers were established with everyone as probable winners.

Then when the League was settled, Hearts seemed simply to be going to make up the numbers for a rather special Ibrox celebration party.

Everyone who supported Rangers thought that – except Manager Jock Wallace. Somewhere that week as the team prepared a niggle of doubt began to rise. There was no logical reason for it and he knew that himself but it was there. He simply began to wonder if, on the day, his old club Hearts would turn the tables on him.

Once more though, it was Derek Johnstone who ended his wories. He scored after only forty-two seconds and there were no doubts remaining . . .

Rangers won a free kick when Jim Jefferies, asked to shackle Johnstone, fouled him with the first tackle of the game. Tommy McLean swung the free kick into goal right footed and Johnstone rose to smash a header past Jim Cruickshank. Then right on half-time after several incredible misses by Rangers Alex MacDonald scored their second goal. A Bobby McKean corner was only partially cleared by John Gallacher as Colin Jackson challenged him. It broke to MacDonald who slotted it away from twenty yards. Derek Johnstone scored again in eighty-one min-

And the Cup story ended right here in the Hampden stand as captain John Greig receives the trophy from SFA President Rankin Grimshaw. The other player is keeper Peter McCloy.

utes and before the end Rangers allowed Hearts to come into the game for a token goal from Graham Shaw.

Unlike Southampton at Wembley, Hearts had gone exactly the way the bookies – and everyone else – had predicted. They had come to Hampden needing time to settle and they hadn't been given it. They had needed twenty minutes to rid themselves of nerves, to find their feet, to frustrate Rangers a little and then, perhaps, to break into counter-attacks in their own right. They didn't get one solitary minute to pull themselves together. While they were still wondering what it was like to be in a Scottish Cup Final they were a goal down.

It must be some kind of record for a player to score two decisive goals in successive weeks in less than a minute's play each time. At Tannadice a week earlier Johnstone had scored in twenty-five seconds – and that goal gave Rangers the League title. Then at Hampden he slowed down his scoring rate a little to hit the opener in forty-two seconds.

Joked Jock Wallace later: 'Derek's getting a row for that. We can't wait that long for him to get the first goal. It's meant to be quicker. He's slowing down isn't he?'

It was swift enough, though, to win Rangers the Cup. For that goal was the killer to any hopes Hearts had.

It also set the seal on the treble – that prize that only two other Rangers teams had been able to win. Now Wallace's Warriors joined these immortals and the fans would not leave Hampden until they saw the players and the manager come out onto the field with the Cup. Seventy-five thousand of them waited to roar their joy as Wallace and his players drained the Cup of champagne out there on the field.

It was an unforgettable climax.